ROMAN PORTRAITS

ROMAN PORTRAITS

The Flavian-Trajanic Period

William C. McDermott
Anne E. Orentzel

University of Missouri Press
Columbia & London
1979

Library of Congress Cataloging in Publication Data

McDermott, William Coffman, 1907–
    Roman Portraits.

    Bibliography : p. 157
    Includes index.
    1. Rome—History—Flavians, 69–96—Biography.
2. Rome—History—Trajan, 98–117—Biography. 3. Statesmen—
Rome—Biography. 4. Rome—Nobility—Biography.
I. Orentzel, Anne E., 1948–   joint author.
II. Title.
DG291.6.M32 937'.06'0922 [B] 79-1559
ISBN 0-8262-0275-6

To Barbara and Jack,
optimis parentibus

Preface

The idea of a series of essays on men and women of the Flavian-Trajanic period came from my coauthor. As the fifteen essays were written, it became clear that they add perspective for the student of this decisive period in Roman imperial development. Not only are the discussed characters interesting as persons, but their careers allowed us to digress on various significant topics in the social and political factors in the life of imperial Rome.

There is some overlapping among the essays that was inevitable, but also desirable. Chapters I–II, V–VII, XI, XV, and the Selected Bibliography are in the main my work; the other nine chapters are chieflly the work of Anne E. Orentzel, but both of us have worked with the whole volume. There is some divergence of opinion in interpretation; for example, I diverge in my estimate of Hadrian, and to some extent in the use of the portraits of imperial women. Other disagreements are slight.

The introductory essay is not an attempt to write the history of the period, but rather to set the background against which the essays were composed and, especially, to explain why we have followed a revisionist view of Domitian's personality and achievement. Also an explanation is needed to clarify the seeming inconsistency of our treatment of the personality of Pliny the Younger and of the validity of his evidence.

The bibliography is brief and generally confined to readily available books with the exception of some basic research tools and those works that specify the publication of nonliterary material. Within the text of the essays, references to literary, epigraphic, and numismatic material are provided for convenient reference. All tranlsations are our own except for Cary's version of Cassius Dio.

We are grateful to Prof. Allen M. Ward of the University of Connecticut for many excellent suggestions that improved our text, and to the Reverend John J. Welsh of the Pontificio Instituto Biblico in Rome.

The volume is also appropriately dedicated to the parents of Anne E. Orentzel, whose support and encouragement enabled her to engage in the study of this period of history.

W. C. M.
Philadelphia, Pennsylvania
December 1978

Contents

I.

INTRODUCTION

The history of the early Roman Empire, often called the principate, is treated in the ancient sources more on the basis of the personalities of the major protagonists than on a rounded view of political, social, and economic factors. However, the underlying currents in imperial development can be partially assessed from fragments of information supplied by writers not concerned with historical development, such as the poets, and by the technical writers who by an extension of the term are included in the histories of classical literature. Much can be learned from archaeology, but more particularly from the vast collections of inscriptional remains.

As in all periods of history, the classical historians and biographers, as well as those more casually connected with historical materials, were the product of their environment and societal prejudices. Roman history of the period under consideration becomes especially difficult because the literary men were largely either from the senatorial class or from those who were closely connected with it. Thus, our knowledge is only partial because of the large gaps in the works produced and because of the bias in the extant literature. Therefore, assessments of the emperors for whom the sources are most abundant lead to variant conclusions among modern historians.

Of the first six emperors who have comprised the dynasty of Augustus, only the founder has escaped bitter diatribes in ancient and modern accounts. And even Augustus, especially for his early years when he was fighting for power in a series of civil wars, has been criticized. Nonetheless, in general he has been praised as a farsighted statesman who established an order of imperial control that benefited the empire and endured for a surprisingly long time.

The ancient picture of Tiberius as an enigmatic ruler who gradually turned out to be a capricious tyrant has been seriously revised by modern scholars who stress the difficulties he encountered, and who admire the efficiency of his provincial administration. The rehabilitation of his principate by modern historians, which at times goes too far, is now rather widely accepted. Under the brief rule of Gaius (Caligula), we can find only few scholars to excuse or admire. More can be said for Claudius, but at the best he failed as a Roman emperor and only partially succeeded in his administration of the provinces.

Nero had notable qualities, most of which were not suitable for imperial power. When he was guided by able advisers, disaster was delayed, but the intensity of the rift between emperor and Senate and his increasing tyranny reached a point where he was literally the last of the Julio-Claudians. His loss of authority over the legions in the provinces led to military control of three men in succession who by vice and vagaries of fortune could not maintain power.

When Vespasian had gained control of the empire, much reorganization was necessary. According to Suetonius (*Vesp.* 1. 1):

> When the empire was for long uncertain and shaken by the rebellion and violent deaths of three emperors finally the Flavian *gens* seized and strengthened it. It was an obscure family without any wax masks of senatorial ancestors, but the state did not need to

regret it although it is clear that Domitian justly paid the penalty for his greed and cruelty.

This passage is a fair appraisal of Vespasian, but it is too harsh in its treatment of Domitian. Vespasian did not conceal the fact that he was founding a dynasty (Suet. *Vesp.* 25) : "My sons will succeed me or no one will." The administration from A.D. 70 to 96 reveals that Trajan continued the same Flavian policy that was followed during that particular period, despite the denigration of the last of the Flavians.

The continuity between the Flavian and the Trajanic ages creates an interesting series of problems in dealing with individuals who bridged the two periods. In the following chapters, this contrast of attitudes, especially between Domitian and Trajan, explains the novelty of our consideration of the individuals described. The imperial regimes, both in discussions of personalities and administrations, have been treated extensively. The subjects of our chapters have been chosen to illustrate and illuminate the background. Most of them have been only casually mentioned or ignored in the general histories.

Because of the fragmentary or conflicting evidence, at times we had to use our imagination and have often reached interpretations that vary with the accepted view of the times. Since the lives of many of these individuals interlocked, some repetition in our essays was unavoidable.

The chief feature of our study is a more favorable view of Domitian than is customary. A full study of the factors involved in the revisionist view of this emperor is peripheral and must await a new study of his character and achievements. However, this volume presents many sidelights that will be germane to such a work. We delineate the lives of a representative group of

3

people who surrounded the emperor and among whom he lived. Their attitudes and prejudices greatly influenced the emperor's thoughts and actions. In addition, our digressions frequently add depth to the social and political institutions of the period.

Moreover, although we have attempted to base our narrative on the ancient source material, this material must be used cautiously, and we have frequently attempted to offer new insights that go beyond the extant sources. Clearly, the subjects of these biographies did not live exactly as portrayed in our essays. But such lives men and women of such rank did live, whether an imperial functionary, empress, imperial mistress, or senator. Their culture, tradition, and intellectual reactions molded their actions.

A few comments on the main sources will clarify the interpretations in these essays. The chief literary sources are Tacitus, Suetonius, Pliny the Younger, and Cassius Dio. For the Julio-Claudian emperors, the material is fairly complete, but that for the Flavians is less adequate. Regarding Nerva and Trajan, the information is extremely scanty, with the exception of the works of Pliny. Casual references by poets and scattered comments by technical writers and the later epitomators occasionally added helpful items. As these authors failed us, more reliance had to be placed on the preserved inscriptions, and fortunately there are many for the period under discussion. Numismatics and archaeology are rarely definitive regarding these particular subjects. As a result, accurate assessment by modern historians becomes difficult.

The account of Tacitus in the *Annals* is almost complete for Tiberius and Nero, but only partial for Claudius. His facts are generally accurate, but his interpretation of Tiberius is marred by innuendo. Of his thirty books, comprising the history of A.D. 14 to 96, apparently twelve discuss the civil wars of 69–70 and the rule of the Flavians. But the *Historiae* are not preserved beyond the first quarter of the fifth book where he was still writing of the year 70. Hence, it is clear that his account of the Flavian dynasty was more of a summary than his history of the Julio-Claudian emperors.

In the extant portion of the *Historiae*, Tacitus treats Vespasian and Titus favorably and is not seriously antagonistic toward Domitian. However, in his biography of his father-in-law Agricola he is bitterly hostile to the last of the Flavians, under whom his career had prospered. He was praetor in 88, already of·the Fifteen men, and from 90 to 93 on provincial assignments as *praetorius*. It is fair to say that he displays the same anti-Domitianic prejudice in the latter books that is displayed in the *Agricola*. Herein he would have followed the hostility of that portion of the Senate which became dominant after Domitian's assassination. His higher offices were Trajanic: consul in 97 and proconsul of Asia about 112–113.

Singularly enough Suetonius is much more detailed in the first six biographies of the emperors, each of which is a single book, than in the Flavian biographies that are placed together in the eighth book. Thus, Gaius (Caligula), emperor from 37 to 41, is treated at almost double the length (37 pages in Ihm's *editio maior*) of Domitian, emperor from 81 to 96 (21 pages in Ihm). His account is somewhat more favorable than those of Tacitus and Pliny, *senatores consulares*, and there are some passages that show Domitian in a surprisingly favorable light. In his early years, Suetonius was an attorney but entered an equestrian career that was crowned by his position as *ab epistulis* under Hadrian.

It was formerly assumed that the office under Hadrian was his sole official position, but an inscription from Hippo has proved that he held several important posts earlier, most probably under Trajan. Therefore, he had excellent opportunities to consult imperial documents, and as an equestrian he was not so strongly affected by the senatorial bias against Domitian. Much excellent information in all of his *de vita Caesarum* is marred by his tendency to generalize on single items and by his fondness for repeating scandal, much of which probably was unfounded.

The most frequently cited and in some ways the most acceptable authority in these essays is Pliny the Younger. The nine books of his personal letters, carefully edited for publication, are a fascinating picture of the life of his times, especially of the upper classes in Rome and Italy. The impression they give, and it is not an incorrect view, is of a kindly and generous man, devoted to his family, on friendly terms with men and women of all ages and of various social strata. He could be grateful and devoted to his aging sponsor (Chapter VII : Corellius Rufus), and kindly to his wife's irascible grandfather (Chapter V : Fabatus). He had a pleasing and long-lasting friendship with Voconius Romanus (Chapter XII). As a successful attorney and an honored consular senator, he aided younger men of promise. He was somewhat staid and could be a bit patronizing (Chapter XI : Cornutus Tertullus ; Chapter XIII : Julius Genitor). However, it is obvious that in these letters Pliny is sketching a good public image of himself, both for his contemporaries and for posterity.

Pliny often deserves to be praised as a learned and honorable senator, doing his duty to the state and to his friends. But there is another side to his character and career that accounts for comments in some situations which show him in an unfavorable light, and at best must be attributed to the bias common to a member of the ruling class. Pliny reveals himself as a dynamic and forceful personality. His career is not always in accord with the generally accepted portrait that he encouraged in his published works.

Although Pliny was of an equestrian family, he had

powerful sponsors : his maternal uncle who adopted him and who had held one of the most important equestrian posts at the time of his death (*praefectus classis*, "commander of the fleet") ; Verginius Rufus, consul for the third time under Nerva, and Pliny's guardian (*tutor*) ; Corellius Rufus, a favorite of Nerva. Nonetheless, only his own industry and ability could result in a career of outstanding success. He was liked by Domitian, Nerva, and Trajan, and with imperial backing was elected to the regular offices at the minimum age. Under Domitian, he became praetor and was appointed prefect of the military treasury ; under Nerva and Trajan, he was prefect of the senatorial treasury. After his consulship with Trajan's favor, he became augur, held a major curatorial post and a unique position as imperial governor of Pontus and Bithynia. Also, before he went East to his province he was at least three times a member of Trajan's *consilium*. Had he not died while in his early fifties, he probably would have become proconsul of Asia or Africa.

Pliny's training in oratory was outstanding. He started practice in the centumviral court in his teens, and by the time he was *consularis* he was the premier orator in Rome. He spoke in the Senate with vigor. Domitian chose him to prosecute Baebius Massa ; Trajan had him prosecute Marius Priscus and Caecilius Classicus ; and he later defended two governors of Pontus and Bithynia. Although his *Panegyricus* is the only one in existence, his published orations were quite popular in his own day.

It is clear from his letters and appointments that he was extremely competent in financial matters. His wealth was not great compared to that of some of his contemporaries, but by expert management he was able to be generous to his native Comum and to many of his friends and acquaintances. Throughout his life, he was deeply interested in literature, encouraged his friends in literary pursuits, and in his forties indulged in the writing of light verse.

These observations show that he was a man of many talents with driving ambition and unflagging energy who was engaged in a flourishing legal practice, in heavy and responsible civilian administration, in time-consuming literary pursuits, and in a great many private business affairs of no small import. There is thus a sharp contrast in his activities with the first impression gained from his private letters.

The final problem in analyzing the information in Pliny's works is the reason for his hostility to the memory of Domitian who had highly favored him, as well as his denigration of Domitian's friends (Chapter II: Veiento). A general point was the senatorial fear of those who had prosecuted for treason (*delatores*, such as Regulus, Chapter X). But more specifically, Pliny resented the attack upon a group of his friends in 93 that resulted in the execution or exile of seven of his Stoic friends (*Ep.* 3. 11). They may well have been guilty of plotting against the emperor, but as always in such cases there were elements of doubt. Pliny wrote that he felt he was in danger, but soon thereafter Domitian appointed him to the military treasury. At one point, Pliny noted that a notorious delator had supplied Domitian with an accusation against him, which was found in the emperor's files at the time of his assassination (*Ep.* 7. 27. 14). It is just possible that Pliny was involved in a plot, since accession of Nerva on the very day of the assassination of his predecessor surely implied the knowledge of the plot, or even participation in it, on the part of some members of the Senate.

There is a final possibility. Pliny's *Panegyricus*, doubtless in its short form in the Senate and clearly in the preserved amplified version, is our most notable anti-Domitianic document. In it, Pliny wrote of the contrast between the evil of Domitian and the beneficence of Trajan. This document was circulated largely among members of the Senate and was in some ways an announcement of conciliation between emperor and Senate. Trajan was no less autocratic than Domitian and followed Flavian policies, but he treated the Senate with such affability that he did not fear plots and could thus avoid the cruelty with which Domitian foiled all plots but the last. Pliny must have been aware of Trajan's attitude, but historians have taken his *Panegyricus* too seriously as evidence.

The other source material can be quickly summarized. Cassius Dio, a consular senator over a century later, generally followed the tradition of the senatorial class, and so derogated Domitian and praised Trajan. Unfortunately, his text is preserved only in long excerpts. Here and there some important details are given but do not substantially contribute more than glimpses of the picture. No biography of Nerva or Trajan has been preserved.

The inscriptional evidence varies in quality. Inscriptions raised to a reigning emperor and his family, as well as issues of coins, were part of the creation of a public image. This was true also of public buildings and especially of sculptured reliefs that adorned imperial monuments. Notable examples can be cited—the triumph over Judea in the panels of the archway of the Arch of Titus raised by Domitian; the incredible column of Trajan in his forum; and a series of seven slabs carved with two historical reliefs that were discovered in 1937 in the excavations under the Palazzo Cancelleria Apostolica in Rome.

To interpret the career of Domitian, we can see that in the third slab of the first relief of the series Vespasian rests his right hand on the shoulder of the youthful Domitian. Father and son wear togas and the scene represents Vespasian's return from the East as emperor in A.D. 70. The second relief shows Domitian (replaced after 96 by the head of Nerva) about to set out for the war with the Chatti in 82. These reliefs probably ornamented an arch erected by Domitian late in his reign.

There had been rumors of disaffection in 70 between Vespasian and his younger son, and the chief literary sources denigrate the victory of Domitian in the war with the Chatti. Consequently these reliefs have been labelled as propaganda favoring Domitian, and of course this is correct. However, it is well to remember that propaganda need not be false.

Thus our essays, based as far as possible on the ancient evidence, often contain speculative extension of the known facts. We hope they will be both edifying and amusing.

II.

FABRICIUS VEIENTO

ter consul

The sources stress that Domitian executed senators who were in opposition to his regime. But we seldom read about the high-ranking senators who were favored not only by Domitian but also by his predecessors and successors. Veiento, an adviser to Domitian, is a notable example of a senator who remained in good standing after the emperor's assassination.

The ancestry of Aulus Didius Gallus Fabricius Veiento is uncertain, and his official career, barring his priestly offices and his three consulships, is subject to dispute. However, he was a consular senator of distinction under the Flavian emperors and was notable as adviser and favorite of Domitian.

The quintuple name, attested by an inscription (*ILS* 1010), allows some speculation. Veiento as a cognomen suggests Etruscan origin. In view of the importance of ritual in Etruscan religion and its impact on Rome, such ancestry may also be confirmed by the various priesthoods Veiento held because of his interest in religious rites. Fabricius is a nomen well known in republican days. However, no connection with republican *Veientones* and *Fabricii* can be ascertained. Certainly, there was some connection with Aulus Didius Gallus, who was consul before 37 and consular legate of Britain from 52 to 58. It has also been suggested that Veiento might have been adopted by Gallus. However, since Gallus was *grauis senectute* in 52 (Tac. *Ann.* 12. 40. 4), the alternative that he was the son of Gallus's daughter is a better conjecture. In either case, the influence of Gallus would assure Veiento of senatorial rank. But this connection with Gallus is tenuous, and Veiento may have been only a distant relative and one of the many *novi homines* who became powerful in the early empire.

The first event of his life is in Cassius Dio who had just noted Nero's enthusiasm for the races and race-horses and then continued (Cary *Dio* 61. 6. 2–3) :

> Thereupon the horsebreeders and charioteers, encouraged by this enthusiasm on his part, proceeded to treat both the praetors and the consuls with great insolence ; and Aulus Fabricius, when praetor, finding them unwilling to take part in the contests on reasonable terms, dispensed with their services, and training dogs to draw chariots, introduced them in place of horses. At this the wearers of the White and the Red immediately entered their chariots for the races ; but as the Greens and the Blues would not participate even then, Nero himself furnished the prizes for the horses and the horse-race took place.

Although this excerpt of Dio is dated as of A.D. 54, it does not give a definite date for Veiento's praetorship that could have been as late as 60.

As praetor, Veiento showed an independence of attitude that was part of his character. He was not a delator under Nero or the Flavians, even though modern accounts frequently have made such statements, which are based only on insinuations made in the hostile post-Domitianic sources. The next event, as noted by Tacitus, clears him of such an accusation in Neronian days.

At the beginning of his narrative of the events of 62, Tacitus recounted the recrudescence of charges of treason (*de maiestate*) brought by prosecutors (*delatores*) and wrote with his consistent hostility toward such ac-

tivity (*Ann.* 14. 48–49). The next short chapter concerned Veiento (14. 50):

> Fabricius Veiento was afflicted by a charge which
> was not dissimilar, because he had written many
> rebukes (insults) against senators and priests in those
> books to which he had given the name *Codicilli*.
> Tullius Geminus the prosecutor added that he had
> sold gifts of the emperor and the right of gaining
> offices. For this reason Nero took up the case, and
> when Veiento was convicted he exiled him from Italy
> and ordered his books to be burnt. They were sought
> out and read over and over while they were obtained
> with peril, soon permission to have them brought
> neglect.

It is noteworthy that here Geminus is the delator, and
the charge of selling influence is neither confirmed nor
denied by the consular historian. There is no mention of
delation on the defendant's part. The next chapter
(14. 51) begins, "But with aid diminished for public
ills day by day. . . ." Thus, there is a hint that Veiento's
exile and Nero's suppression of freedom of speech
were among the public ills, and there is an indication that
Veiento was not a delator.

A little more about the nature of the work may be
gained from its title. *Codicilli* might mean "notes," or
"testament (will)," or "rescript." The first is innocuous,
the second satiric, the third is taken from the nomenclature of the imperial chancery. Perhaps, Veiento meant
the title to be ambiguous. I translated *multa et probosa*
as "many rebukes (insults)," and the phrase could be
serious or satiric, but it is not clear whether Tacitus had
direct knowledge of Veiento's text. The phrase *in patres
et sacerdotes* ("against senators and priests") means
that he wrote barbed comments against the ignorance or
venality of senators who held priestly offices.

It is surprising that the emperor sat as judge in a case that was not very important. It could be assumed that the charge of selling influence because of favor in court circles was the reason, but this charge by Geminus was probably false. Nero, especially in his earlier years, paid little attention to hostile remarks, whether oral or written (Suet. *Nero* 39), although later inadvertent words were made, the basis for a charge of treason (ibid., 32. 2). Hence, at first glance Veiento's *Codicilli* do not seem an adequate reason for exile, even though Nero's sentence was comparatively mild.

The structure of senatorial priesthoods itself allows some speculation. There were four great colleges of priests restricted to senatorial members: the Pontiffs, the Augurs, the Fifteen for Sacred Rites, and the Seven for Sacred Banquets. Each emperor was chief pontiff (*pontifex maximus*) heading the state religion and was also a member of the other three colleges. Veiento, although still only *praetorius*, could probably have been already a member of the third college whose duties required extensive religious knowledge since they consulted the Sibylline books in important crises and participated in deciding which non-Roman deities could be accepted for Roman worship. Veiento's probable Etruscan background would have qualified him for such a post even though membership in important priesthoods was usually restricted to young men of more distinguished rank. Thus, early appointment of Veiento seems likely.

If Veiento had been already one of the Fifteen, Nero would well have considered the *Codicilli* as a violation of the secrecy of sacerdotal matters and may have felt that this work was a personal attack upon the emperor. If so, it would explain his exile of Veiento because it is obvious from Suetonius that Nero was at times a victim of religious and superstitious terrors (*Nero* 46).

Veiento returned from exile after Nero's death, either during the civil wars or after Vespasian had consolidated his rule. He became consul some time after 70 and may have become a member of the imperial council, although that is not confirmed until Domitian becomes the emperor. A military diploma (*CIL* 16. 158) dates his second consulship to 80, suffect for the Emperor Titus.

It is probable that at least under the Flavians Veiento did serve as an official in the provinces and in Italy, but the evidence of a full listing of his *cursus honorum* is lacking. A fragmentary acephalous inscription from Arles (*AE* 1952, 168) has been assigned to him, but this is speculative and has been challenged. If the ascription is correct, Veiento was at one time a provincial governor. However, his real importance, especially in the reign of Domitian, was as trusted adviser to the emperor.

The fourth satire of Juvenal, published about fifteen years after Domitian's assassination, is an attack upon that emperor. When a huge turbot was caught in the Adriatic and presented to the emperor, he is pictured as calling a full meeting of his imperial council (*consilium principis*) to discuss the destiny of the fish, as if it were an important matter of governmental policy. His councillors (*amici Caesaris*) appear and one by one are satirized as fearful, or venal, or bloodthirsty. Veiento was a member of the council, and undoubtedly the evidence of the satirist is a historical fact.

In line 112, "Prudent Veiento (enters) with death-dealing Catullus." Even Juvenal could not avoid the adjective *prudens*, but he tempered praise by linking him with the hated Catullus Messalinus (guilt by association) and by placing sycophantic words in his mouth (123–29):

> Veiento does not yield, but as if a fanatic stung by
> your gadfly, Bellona, he says: "You have a mighty
> omen of a great and brilliant triumph. You will
> capture some king, or Arviragus will fall from his
> British chariot. The monster is foreign: do you see

the spear-like fins erect on its back?" The only thing missing for Fabricius was naming the origin and age of the turbot.

Here the satirist based his passage on Veiento's priestly interests.

Without evidence it would be a safe conjecture that elements in this mockery of Domitian's council were a parody of an earlier pro-Domitianic work. Happily an early editor using an ancient note (on 4. 94) quoted four lines from the *de bello Germanico* of Statius:

> (Catullus Messalinus deprived of his) eyes, the mild
> wisdom of Nestorian Crispus and Fabius Veiento—
> the purple marked each as powerful, thrice they
> filled the reminding fasti—and Acilius almost a
> neighbor of the palace of Caesar.

Since the dangling *lumina* of the first line must refer to Catullus, four *amici Caesaris* appear in these lines. The "mild wisdom" (*mitis prudentia*) of Crispus and Veiento is further marked when the poet compares Crispus to the aged Nestor of Homer and changes Fabricius to Fabius, with reference to Fabius Maximus Cunctator, the chief mentor of the Roman Senate in the Second Punic War. Statius's praise of Domitian as expressed in his extant *Silvae* has usually been considered servile flattery, but a good case can be made of it as genuine admiration. If such be true, then his estimate of Veiento expresses the poet's real feeling.

Statius's epic surely concerned the war with the Chatti that was won by Domitian in the summer of 83, and the four-line fragment would then be the poetic version of Domitian's council at which strategy was planned. Veiento was most probably *comes* during the time that the emperor was in command. Such a position was not military but advisory as befitted the aging consular senator. The emperor's triumph and assumption of the honorary title of *Germanicus* (*cognomen ex virtute*) would then occur late in 83. Veiento's third consulship, and probably that of Vibius Crispus, may well have coincided with the triumphal celebration. If so, they had an important official role in the festivities that had a strong religious overtone.

An inscription was found at Mainz in Upper Germany at the confluence of the Main and the Rhine rivers, a natural site for Domitian's headquarters in the war (*ILS* 1010) :

> Aulus Didius Gallus Fabricius Veiento, thrice consul,
> a member of the College of Fifteen for Sacred Rites,
> priest of Augustus, of the Flavians, of Titus Tatius,
> and Attica his wife rightly and freely paid their vow
> to Nematona.

This dedication was probably Veiento's last action before returning to Rome. It reflects the fulfillment of a vow made for the successful completion of the war. Nematona, a Gallic goddess whose name is elsewhere linked with Mars (*ILS* 4586), reminds us of Bellona in Juvenal's parody.

This combination of four priesthoods is unique. The major office (as one of the *quindecimviri sacris faciendis*) had probably been gained under Nero before Veiento's exile in 62. The three lesser priesthoods (*sodalitates*) cannot be firmly dated but seem to be in chronological order. Hence, he may have become priest of Augustus under Nero, the last of the Julio-Claudians. It is safe to assume that he became priest of the Flavians after Vespasian's death, possibly when a consul for the second time in 80. Honors for Titus after his death would fall within the duties of this second office. I would take his third minor priesthood as an office to honor Titus Tatius the Sabine king, who, according to legend, and after the seizure of the Sabine women, becomes a colleague of Romulus.

Veiento's religious offices linked him closely with

Domitian, who was the first emperor since Augustus to display an intense interest in religious observance. Moreover, he was more sincere in his beliefs than the coolly calculating Augustus had been. This fact is supported by both literary and archaeological evidence. Two chapters in Suetonius outline some of his activities (*Dom.* 4–5). Some of the items are of special interest here:

> He gave the secular games, with the time computed not to the year in which Claudius gave them most recently, but to the year in which Augustus had formerly given them. . . . He established a triple quinquennial contest in honor of Capitoline Jupiter. . . . He presided at the contest with sandals, draped in a crimson cloak of the Greek type, wearing a golden crown upon his head with the likeness of Jupiter, Juno, and Minerva, and there sat with him the priest of Jupiter and the college of Flavian priests in like apparel except that his likeness was on their crowns. . . . He erected also a temple of the Flavian *gens.*

The priest of Jupiter (*flamen Dialis*) was the most important priest outside of the four great colleges, and together with the chief Vestal he sat with the College of Pontiffs when it met in plenary session. There is no evidence for the total number of Flavian priests (*Flaviales*).

One inscription especially reveals Domitian's religious interests, a charter for a consecrated area (*ILS* 4914):

> This open space, closed within the limits of pillars by a spear-like fence, with the altar below, was dedicated by the Emperor Caesar Domitian Augustus Germanicus in accordance with a vow, because it had been long neglected and not restored. (It was set aside) for the sake of warding off fires when the city burned for nine days in Neronian times. It has been dedicated under these conditions, that within the limits no one shall be permitted to erect a building, to live, to do business, to plant a tree, or to sow

anything, and that the praetor to whom this region
has fallen by lot, or some other magistrate on the
Vulcanalia on the tenth day before the Kalends of
September every year with a red calf and a red boar
and with prayers. . . . This the Emperor Caesar
Domitian Augustus Germanicus, chief pontiff,
decided . . . should be done.

After the great fire in 64 (Tac. *Ann.* 15. 38–45), Nero
had ordered in accordance with the Sibylline books
expiatory sacrifices, including one to Vulcan, and had
ordered open spaces to prevent further fires. However,
this specific open space (*area*) and the altar to the god
of fire were not mentioned by the historian. Restrictions
were apparently neglected until Domitian acted.

The devastating fire of 64 occurred in the latter half
of July (Tac. *Ann.* 15. 41. 2) at which time Domitian
was thirteen. Whether Vespasian had returned from
Africa or not (he was proconsul in the early sixties) the
teenage youngster would have been living then in Rome
or on one of his family's country estates. The holocaust
made a great impression on him. Veiento had been exiled
from Italy in 62 but was probably already a member
of the College of Fifteen and had a double interest in the
event. Tacitus gives this item (*Ann.* 44. 1):

Expiatory rites to the gods were sought and the
Sibylline books were consulted, and in accordance
with them supplication was made to Vulcan and Ceres
and Proserpina, and Juno was propitiated by matrons,
first on the Capitoline, then at the nearest sea whence
water was drawn and sprinkled on the temple and the
statue of the goddess. Also women who had husbands
performed the *sellisternia* and vigils.

Domitian's charter, quoted above, cannot be specifically
dated. I assume that Domitian's vow was made at the
time when he escaped death late in the year 69, when the
Capitoline was burnt in the conflict between the troops

of Vitellius and those who favored Vespasian (Tac. *Hist.* 3. 71–74). Fulfillment of the vow would then take place soon after Domitian's return from the German border, and the emperor repaired the neglect of his father and brother and instituted these rites to Vulcan in an area on the Quirinal near Vespasian's house where he had been born.

I have assumed the presence of Veiento at the annual celebrations of the Vulcanalia to be on 23 August. Suetonius confirms that he appeared with Domitian at the quinquennial contest honoring Capitoline Jupiter (*agon Capitolinus*), which was established in 86 and which was similar to the Greek games. The main contests were in poetry and eloquence in both Greek and Latin, in music, and athletics. There he presided, wearing the costume of those who gave games in the Greek East. These contests were in accordance not only with his religious interests but also with his intellectual bent since according to Quintilian he had a considerable reputation as a poet before becoming emperor (10. 1. 91): ". . . Care over the earth turned Germanicus Augustus from the studies he had started, and it seemed to the gods too little that he be the greatest of poets." The effigies of the Capitoline triad on his crown were appropriate since he was especially devoted to Jupiter and Minerva. The priest of Jupiter (*flamen Dialis*) sat with him and all of the *Flaviales*, wearing similar garments and crowns with the emperor's effigy. Prizes were awarded "by all the votes of the judges" according to an inscription on the sixth agon in 106 (*ILS* 5178).

It is ironic that Trajan's father Marcus Ulpius Traianus, consul in 69 or 70, and finally proconsul of Asia 79–80, was both *Flavialis* and a member of the College of Fifteen (*ILS* 8970). If he survived to 86, he was one of Domitian's attendants at the agon. However, Veiento was clearly present, not only in 86 but also in 90 and 94 at the second and third contests. He may have supervised the arrangements. Considering the functions of the College of Fifteen, this elder statesman had a comprehensive knowledge of Roman and non-Roman ritual and religion. These contests were continued under Trajan, but the warrior emperor was not enthusiastic, for his most notable public spectacle was the bloody gladiatorial contest that he staged to celebrate his Dacian conquest. These combats lasted through most of the summer and fall of 109 as is attested by a notice in a fragment of the Calendar of Ostia (*FO* 22. 12–14) : "On the Kalends of November the Emperor Trajan completed his gladiatorial games in 117 days with 4,941–½ pairs."

In the year 47, in which Claudius celebrated the secular games, Tacitus relates the following (*Ann.* 11. 11. 1) :

> Under the same consuls, the secular games were viewed in the eight hundredth year after the founding of Rome and in the sixty-fourth year after Augustus had given them. I pass over the calculations of each emperor since they are sufficiently related in the books which I composed on the deeds of the Emperor Domitian. For he too gave secular games and I was present with greater interest since I was a member of the College of Fifteen and was then praetor. I relate this not as a boast but because of old the College of Fifteen Men and the magistrates particularly perform the ceremonial duties.

The portion of the *Historiae* in which this account appeared is not extant.

The secular games of Augustus in 17 B.C. are well known because fragments of the minutes are preserved and Horace's *Secular Hymn* is available. For three days and nights, there were religious celebrations, honoring Fates, Jupiter and Juno, Apollo, and Diana. On the night of 31 May–1 June, Augustus sacrificed. The following passage gives this account of the high, holy character of the ritual (*ILS* 5050, lines 91–97) :

He prayed in this manner: "Fates! Because of the instructions that were written with reference to you in the Sibylline books and that it may be of greater benefit to the Roman citizens, let the sacrifice be made to you of nine female lambs and nine female goats. I beg you and beseech you that you increase the empire and majesty of the Roman citizens in war and at home, that the Latins always obey, and that you grant eternal victory and well-being to the Roman citizens and the legions of Roman citizens and hold safe the state of Roman citizens, that you be of good will and propitious toward the Roman citizens, the College of Fifteen Men, me, my house, my family."

Marcus Agrippa was deuteragonist to the emperor in these rites.

Claudius set the *saeculum* at 100 years, instead of the 110 years reckoned by Augustus, and his games were the cause of ironic comment (Suet. *Claud.* 21. 2):

Wherefore the voice of the herald was mocked when in solemn manner he invited them to games "which no one had seen, or would see," since there were present those who had seen them.

However, the prize jest was that of Lucius Vitellius, thrice consul, censor, and father of an emperor, who said to Claudius: "May you do this often" (Suet. *Vit.* 2. 5).

Details on the games of 88 are lacking but some suppositions are possible. By this year, Veiento may have been the senior member of the College of Fifteen, either in age, service, or both. Surely the emperor, who was also a member of the College of Fifteen, consulted with him about the Sibylline books and assigned him to plan the details of the ritual and to supervise the preparations. Probably there was close consultation between the two men, and in the religious rites Veiento was second only to Domitian, as Marcus Agrippa had been to Augustus.

Another point is made by Suetonius (*Dom.* 4. 3):

"At these games on the day of the games in the circus, so that a hundred starts might be completed, he reduced each race from seven laps to five." His statement fits Domitian's enthusiasm for the races that exhibited the training of the horses and the skill of the drivers (*aurigae*). Suetonius's general comments on Domitian's presentation of games indicate his preference of the races to gladiatorial contests (*Dom.* 4. 1–2). Few gladiators survived to receive the headless spear (*rudis*) of discharge. The racing driver was subject to accidents, but not too frequently, if we may judge by the career of Gaius Appuleius Diocles in the days of Hadrian who survived 4,257 races (*ILS* 5287).

The *templum gentis Flaviae* was erected on the site of Vespasian's house on the Quirinal where Domitian had been born (Suet. *Dom.* 1. 5). This magnificent building was a symbol of Rome's enduring power, and a mausoleum for the Flavians. It was dedicated in the middle nineties, since there are references in Martial (9. 1. 8; 3. 12, 20) and in Statius (*Silv.* 4. 3. 18–19; 5. 1. 240–41) whose poems date to 94–95. However, since the structure would also link Domitian with his deified father and brother, the plans for the erection were surely developed early in his reign. At some time, probably before the dedication, the ashes of Vespasian and Titus and of other deceased Flavians were placed there. There were ceremonial observances at this shrine on many occasions before 94. At all of these, the members of the *Collegium Flavialium*, including Veiento, would participate in the religious rites with the emperor.

The last known burial in the mausoleum is noted by Suetonius (*Dom.* 17. 3):

He (Domitian) was killed on the fourteenth day
before the Kalends of October. . . . His body was
carried out by the undertakers in a cheap coffin and
Phyllis his nurse held the funeral in her suburban
villa on the Latin road, but she secretly placed his

relics in the Temple of the Flavian *gens* and mixed
them with the ashes of Julia, daughter of Titus whom
she had also raised.

Despite the Senate's curse on Domitian's memory
(*damnatio memoriae*), the new emperor Nerva may
have quietly allowed Phyllis the tribute to the man whom
she had suckled as a babe. Could Veiento, still *Flavialis*,
have advised Nerva and been present? Domitia Longina,
who survived her husband and who continued to list
herself as "the wife of Domitian" (she never remarried), may also have been granted burial in this mausoleum by Hadrian.

Veiento's apparently extensive religious participation
in the councils of the emperor, the fact that he was an
official *amicus principis,* his third consulship, and his
accumulation of religious offices, all mark him as one of
the most important men under the third Flavian. The
importance of his third consulship calls for further
elaboration. Pliny in writing to his friend Voconius
Romanus on the death of his beloved guardian Verginius
Rufus said: "He held a third consulship so that he
gained the highest rank of a private individual" (*Ep. 2.
1. 2*). Here *privatus* means a senator who is not emperor
or of the imperial family. Before 96, only four men
(*privati*) were *ter consul*: Lucius Vitellius under
Claudius (47); Licinius Mucianus, the king-maker
under Vespasian (72); Veiento and Vibius Crispus
under Domitian (83?). From 97 to 100 (under Nerva
and Trajan), this honorable position was lowered in
esteem when given to: Verginius Rufus (97), Julius
Frontinus (100), Vestricius Spurinna (100). Licinius
Sura (107) was as deserving as the first four and was
the last senator outside the imperial household to be so
honored.

For a time under Nerva, Veiento attempted to exercise his influence. An instance is recorded in a letter that
Pliny addressed a decade later to his young friend

Ummidius Quadratus (9. 13) who had a distinguished career under Hadrian. Pliny, already *praetorius* and notable as an orator in the Senate and the centumviral court, brashly decided to attack Publicius Certus who had aided in 93 in the downfall and execution of the younger Helvidius Priscus, a member of a Stoic circle that was in opposition to Domitian. In a Senate meeting, Pliny broached the topic out of order and was shouted down. Among others who spoke against him was Veiento. Most of the senators preferred not to see one of their own class attacked.

But when Pliny had the floor, he delivered a full-scale oration that he later published, and his eloquence won over the Senate. Then only Veiento attempted to defend Certus but was interrupted by shouts. He made a point of order and said: "I beg, senators, that you do not force me to ask for the aid of the tribunes" (19). Then the tribune Murena (that is, Pompeius Falco) said: "Most distinguished Veiento, I permit you to speak." His action was of no avail since the presiding consul adjourned the meeting amid turmoil.

Had Veiento been of another culture he might have quoted: "How are the mighty fallen! Tell it not in Gath, publish it not in the streets of Askelon." But instead he complained of the insult in the words with which Diomedes addressed the aged Nestor (*Il.* 8. 102): "Old man, truly young warriors ill oppress thee" (20). Even though a majority of the Senate by the end of his speech approved of Pliny's project, Veiento had his way, for Nerva did not allow a prosecution (22). Perhaps Veiento was in Nerva's *consilium*. This session of the Senate was held in December of 96.

In another letter written somewhat earlier (104 or 105), Pliny harks back to Nerva's short reign (4. 22. 4–6):

> Nerva was dining with a few men; Veiento was reclining next to him, and even in his bosom: I have

said everything when I named the man. Conversation turned to Catullus Messalinus who deprived of his eyesight added the ills of blindness to his savage character. . . . All were speaking at dinner in common of his wickedness and his bloodthirsty votes, when the emperor himself said: "What do you think he would have suffered if he were alive?" And Mauricus said: "He would be dining with us."

Junius Mauricus had been exiled in 93 and his brother Arulenus Rusticus executed. Both were friends of Pliny, Stoics, and bitter enemies of Domitian. Nerva was apparently trying to reconcile unsuccessfully two factions. Pliny spoke in admiration of Mauricus, but even Stoic harshness could not excuse Mauricus's blatant insult to his host and to Nerva's most important guest. Pliny adds to the insult by his innuendo that Catullus and Veiento were linked in bloodthirsty actions. This dinner probably took place after the Senate meeting since Pliny noted elsewhere that Mauricus was dilatory in returning from exile (*Ep.* 1. 5. 16). I would suggest that Nerva found it politic to break with Veiento when he adopted Trajan in the fall of 97. We do not know how long Veiento survived, but he probably moved in 97 to his suburban estates.

By conjectures based on fragmentary evidence, we can follow a career of a man who rose to a position of great influence and then found his power ephemeral. Such is the fate of a statesman whose importance is based on another man's favor.

III.

ANTONIA CAENIS

concubina imperatrix

Antonia Caenis is a highly attractive and fascinating character. Unfortunately, nothing is known of her origins. She may have been a home-born slave, or a Greek slave. However, her talents that included an eidetic memory (Dio 66. 14. 1–2) won her a high place in the household of the younger Antonia, mother of the Emperor Claudius, for she became one of her secretaries. The position was one of considerable importance, for it involved the drafting of important correspondence and gave Caenis access to the secrets of the imperial circle. She performed her duties discreetly and efficiently, stayed in the service of Antonia, and enjoyed her patroness' complete confidence. Caenis was the one whom Antonia employed in 31 when she wrote to Tiberius, staying at Capri, that Sejanus's intrigues were less than disinterested. Afterwards, she ordered Caenis to erase the drafts, whereupon Caenis replied: "You order me to no avail, my lady, for this and all else which you dictate to me is engraved in my mind and impossible to erase" (Dio 66. 14. 2–3). Any other slave or freedwoman might have been killed for so bold a statement, but Antonia did not mind. She believed that Caenis could be trusted to keep a secret. It may be guessed that when Antonia died on 1 May 37 (*FO* 10. 20–21) Caenis received a handsome legacy in recognition of her services. It is then likely that she remained in the imperial household where she would have been given a post suitable for her talents.

It must have been her position, the fact that she was a confidante of the powerful imperial circle, that initially attracted Vespasian to her. Although from an undistinguished family of Reate in the Sabine area, already under Tiberius he was tribune of the soldiers and quaestor, by 38 aedile and by 40 praetor at the age of thirty-one. Such rapid progress needed ability and a friend in imperial circles. Accordingly, he courted Caenis, who welcomed his flattery (Suet. *Vesp.* 3). Her position as Antonia's secretary was a lonely one. Her erudition and intelligence would certainly have set her apart from the majority of fellow slaves and freedwomen, but at that time she could hardly converse as an equal with her imperial masters. Since she held a position more important than was ordinarily granted to a freedwoman, she probably aroused some suspicion in the imperial entourage. Fortunately, she had a powerful friend in Narcissus who may have been a freedman of Antonia and who under Claudius was secretary for imperial correspondence (*libertus ab epistulis*). His service under Tiberius and Gaius is not recorded, but it is safe to assume that it must have been of significant importance. Caenis may have been his assistant after the death of Antonia since her competence is so well attested.

However, what may have begun as a calculated and mercenary conquest on Vespasian's part resulted in his falling deeply in love with Caenis, a love that she returned. Caenis had many fine qualities to retain his affection, an attractive face and figure, a dynamic and vibrant personality, erudition, and a keen political insight. Although the somewhat puritanical historian, Cassius Dio, bluntly calls her a concubine, he respectfully notes that she was exceedingly faithful and that Vespasian took excessive delight in her (66. 14. 1). There

is no question that Vespasian would have married her if
she had been of higher rank. It may be guessed that she
worked untiringly on his behalf and brought him to
the notice of Narcissus whose favor and influence secured him important offices (Suet. *Vesp.* 4. 1–2).

Although Vespasian married Flavia Domitilla in
Gaius's reign, he does not seem to have completely
broken relations with Caenis. Their relationship would
not have been criticized in Roman society, for the keep-
ing of a slave or freedwoman as concubine by a senator
was so common that it would attract no notice. Furthermore, Vespasian's wife was in no position to object.
Before her marriage, she had been Statilius Capella's
mistress, an African knight from Sabrata [*sic*] (Suet.
Vesp. 3). Vespasian's sons do not seem to have resented
Caenis. Titus could hardly criticize his father's love for
Caenis, for as a young man he had acquired an unenviable reputation for hard drinking and profligacy.
He had a passion for eunuchs and boys, while his liaison
with Queen Berenice scandalized the aristocracy (Suet.
Tit. 7. 1; Dio 66. 15. 4). Domitian is not believed to
have been on good terms with her, but the truth may be
otherwise. It is unlikely that he resented her, for his
own mother had died when he was quite young and he
could hardly have turned a blind eye to his father's
actions. Suetonius, to illustrate Domitian's discourtesy
and presumption, tells how when Caenis returned from
Istria, she offered her cheek as usual for Domitian to
kiss, but he held out his hand instead (*Dom.* 12. 3). Yet,
if this incident took place after Vespasian became emperor, Domitian's conduct becomes clear. His father
was now emperor, and imperial protocol demanded that
he not be so intimate with a freedwoman.

During the greater part of Nero's reign, Vespasian
was in debt and out of favor (Suet. *Vesp.* 4. 3–4).
Caenis may have come to his aid and advanced him

money, as well as using all the influence she had at court to see that his name was considered in the matter of the Judean command. Her loyalty and devotion were rewarded many times over when Vespasian returned from the East as emperor. He called her to court and accorded her every honor save the title of wife (Suet. *Vesp.* 3). Caenis had become empress de facto.

Cassius Dio declares that she used her influence to amass enormous wealth by selling governorships, procuratorships, generalships, priesthoods, and even imperial decisions with the suspected connivance of the emperor (66. 14. 3–4). This is unlikely. Although Caenis must have been approached by many people seeking favors and positions and given rich gifts or money, which was the fashion of ancient diplomacy, Vespasian seems to have kept his own counsel. Throughout his reign, Vespasian had an excellent reputation for justice and for his choice of capable officials and advisers (Suet. *Vesp.* 9–10, 17). Undoubtedly, he did listen with respect when Caenis recommended some person or course of action, but she does not appear to have influenced him regarding major policies and decisions. Caenis, like Nero's freedwoman concubine, Acte, did become extremely wealthy and owned many slaves (*CIL* 6. 15110, 18358, 20950), but she does not appear to have been hated by the senatorial class which would indicate that her position, like that of Acte, was quite unobtrusive and involved no real voice in government.

Although Caenis reached great heights, she did not enjoy her good fortune for any great length of time, for she died some time between 71 and 75 (Dio 66. 14. 1). Vespasian must have grieved deeply, for though he eventually replaced her with several mistresses, none succeeded in holding his affection to the extent that Caenis did or had her name bequeathed to posterity (Suet. *Vesp.* 21).

Her sepulchral inscription (*titulus sepulchralis*) is

preserved (*CIL* 6. 12037). As in life, so in death, her imperial connections were not flaunted. This modest statement was carved on a marble altar:

Sacred to the deified shade of Antonia Caenis, freedwoman of Augusta. Aglaus, her freedman, with Aglaus and Gline and Aglais his children (erected this altar) to his best patroness.

A generation earlier, the Emperor Gaius had granted his grandmother Antonia the title of *Augusta*, which was properly used in the epitaph of Caenis.

From the days of the Emperor Augustus, the male slaves (*servi*) and freedmen (*liberti*) of the imperial household (*familia Caesaris*) assumed an important part in the civil administration of the empire. Some emperors, such as Domitian and Trajan, controlled them strictly; others, notably Claudius, gave them such power and wealth that they were more influential than most of the senators. This influence of the male members of the *familia Caesaris* is often emphasized, but mention of the women is infrequent. The career of Caenis reveals how women with talent and discretion could gain real influence. Earlier Caenis smoothed the way for Vespasian's advancement. Later she was rewarded by his respect and affection and became almost empress (*paene imperatrix*).

IV.
BERENICE

paene imperatrix

Whenever Berenice is mentioned by the imperial historians, there is always an accompanying ripple of disgust. She was regarded as a Jewish Cleopatra, who nearly brought her Mark Antony, in this case the Emperor Titus, to ruin. However, it was Berenice's misfortune to be born a woman in a man's world that could not accept her ability and ambition.

Josephus tells us that Berenice was sixteen when her father, Herod Agrippa, died (*AJ* 19. 354) in the year 44, so her date of birth would be in the year 28. Nothing is known of her childhood. Her father spent most of his time in political intrigue and avoiding his creditors. However, he was a cultured man who enjoyed the friendship of Claudius and his mother, the younger Antonia. Berenice probably accompanied him and her mother, Cypros, on their journeys and met many of the important personages of the day. Presumably, she received the best education possible, for the fact that she was able to fascinate Titus, a man of considerable intellectual attainments, indicates that she was an extremely accomplished woman.

When Berenice was thirteen, her father gave her in marriage to Marcus Julius Alexander, son of Alexander Alabarch, who was one of Herod Agrippa's political allies. But the bridegroom died shortly after the marriage, and Berenice's father quickly found another husband for her. This time he chose her uncle, Herod, who ruled the rich and important client state of Chalcis (Joseph. *AJ* 19. 276; *BJ* 2. 217, 221). The marriage seems to have been satisfactory, for there is no hint of any domestic scandal and Berenice fulfilled her duty by bearing two sons, Berenicianus and Hyrcanus. However, Herod died in 48 or 49. Claudius reduced Chalcis to provincial status and sent procurators who were forbearing enough to respect local customs and were content to keep the peace (Joseph. *AJ* 20. 104). It is unlikely that Berenice demurred at the imperial settlement, for she must have realized that the local aristocracy and populace would never have tolerated a woman as ruler. She seems to have been happy to return to the house of her brother, Herod Agrippa II, who now ruled Judea.

During her marriage to Herod of Chalcis, Berenice must have grown remarkably in political and intellectual insight. Her brother recognized her abilities, for she soon occupied a position of joint-ruler. She was called "great queen . . . descendant of great kings, benefactors of this city" on one inscription in Athens (*IG* 2/3² 3449), and when she and her brother named the temple built by Herod the Great, she is described as "the offspring of the great king" (*AE* 1928, 82). Josephus regarded them as joint-sovereigns (*Vit.* 49. 180–81), and even Tacitus addressed her as Queen Berenice (*Hist.* 2. 2. 1; 81. 2). Her influence was considerable. Once she interceded for the life of Justus, a rebel and a rival historian of Josephus. Although Herod wished to have the man executed, he yielded to his sister's pleas, commuted the sentence to imprisonment, and eventually pardoned Justus completely, making him his secretary (Joseph. *Vit.* 343, 355). Josephus seems to have been completely disgusted at the turn of events. He hated Justus to the point of obsession and may have been equally furious at Berenice for not letting Herod put his rival out of the way. This incident may explain why Josephus is so hostile in his treatment of Berenice.

During the next fifteen years, Berenice remained at her brother's court, presumably as one of his chief advisers. She accompanied him in 60 when he went to greet the new governor, Porcius Festus, and heard St. Paul plead his case at Caesarea (*Acts* 25–26). Agrippa regarded Paul's strenuous attempt to convert him with amusement and laconically remarked: "Almost thou persuadest me to be a Christian" (26. 28). Berenice probably thought as her brother did.

However, Herod's affection and high respect for his sister were to have some unfortunate consequences. Drusilla, his younger sister, resented Berenice's dominance, and the two women quarreled bitterly. Josephus declared that Drusilla married the procurator of Judea, Antonius Felix, who was also the brother of Claudius's freedman, Pallas, to avoid Berenice's spiteful treatment (*AJ* 20. 143). Furthermore, the closeness of brother and sister gave rise to extremely ugly rumors that the two were having incestuous relations (Joseph. *AJ* 20. 145; Juv. 6. 156–58). In 65, Berenice hastily married King Polemo of Cilicia to stop the story. Apparently, Polemo thought Berenice a great matrimonial prize, for he even underwent circumcision in order to marry into the family of Herod. However, the marriage was a failure. Josephus states quite bluntly that she deserted Polemo out of sheer licentiousness (*AJ* 20. 145–46). Yet the case may be otherwise. Polemo may have indulged in intrigues or meddled with Berenice's money and property.

Judea had always been a difficult province for the Romans to govern, since there was continual strife between Pharisees and Sadducees, Greeks and Jews. There were also the Christians to be reckoned with and rioting always flared up at the first sign of weakness in Roman authority, for the Jews had never given up their dream of national independence. The exactions of the governor, Gessius Florus, are credited with starting the great rebellion in 66. When Florus encountered resistance in Jerusalem, he ordered the soldiers to slaughter the populace. Berenice was in the city to discharge a vow for a recent recovery but probably to keep an eye on the political situation as well. Putting aside all regal pride, she begged Florus to spare the people, but Florus scorned her efforts and forced her to watch the killing and torture perpetrated by his soldiers. He would have had her killed as well, but, fortunately, her guard protected her (Joseph. *BJ* 2. 310–14).

Berenice's complaint to Cestius Gallus, governor of Syria, was ineffectual (ibid., 2. 333). She and her brother made every attempt to stop the impending revolt. Herod tried to reason with the people, pointing out the futility of fighting a successful war against the Romans, while Berenice used a woman's arguments, tears. However, passions were too inflamed and the Zealots won the day and amused themselves by burning Agrippa's and Berenice's palaces (ibid., 2. 402–6, 426).

It must have been clear to both that there was only one practical course of action, to leave the country until order was restored by the Romans. They escaped safely, but their chief minister, Ptolemy, was waylaid and robbed of all his baggage, which included a large amount of clothing, many silver goblets, and six hundred gold coins. The booty was brought to none other than Josephus, who declared that he condemned the bandits' acts and planned to restore the treasure to its rightful owners, but the intrigues of his archenemy, John of Gischala, prevented him (ibid., 2. 598–619). But he was not influenced by such scruples when he plundered Berenice's granaries (*Vit.* 119).

In 67, Vespasian was given the Judean command and went East with his son, Titus. It was only natural that he would want to meet the client king and his sister in order to consult with them and to ask their advice about the present situation. Titus appears to have been charmed with Berenice from the very first. His attraction to her might be regarded with some surprise, for she was more than ten years his senior. But young men often find older women attractive, especially if they are vivacious and charming. Berenice was not a particularly beautiful woman. A bronze portrait bust in the Naples Museum that has been tentatively identified as that of Berenice shows a rather plump woman with unexciting classical features. Yet, Titus may have been impressed by her vibrant personality, her energy, her erudition, her intellectual and political insight. She, in turn, could not fail to be impressed by Titus, for Vespasian's older son was an extremely dashing and dynamic young soldier (Suet. *Tit.* 3–4; Dio 66. 4–5). Since she was no longer a young woman, she must have found his attentions both flattering and welcome.

When Vespasian made his bid for empire, Berenice and her brother supported the Flavian cause wholeheartedly. Both must have realized that the energetic Vespasian would soon defeat the indolent Vitellius. Furthermore, through Vespasian they might regain their kingdom. Berenice presented the elderly Vespasian with rich gifts, an act that charmed him, and proceeded to promote his cause ardently (Tac. *Hist.* 2. 81. 2). Herod and Berenice had calculated correctly at every turn: Judea was subdued, the Flavians were victorious, and the dynasty of Herod won back its kingdom.

Berenice and her brother visited Rome in 75. Once more Titus fell under her spell. Dio declares that she was at the height of her power. Agrippa was awarded the title of honorary praetor, while Berenice dwelt in the palace, living with Titus as his wife. She was convinced that they would marry and was already acting as empress-to-be (66. 15. 3–4). Apparently, there may have been some talk that they had married, for the author of the *Epitome de Caesaribus* does refer to Berenice as Titus's wife (10. 4). However, the intended match was not popular in Roman society. Vespasian may have disapproved. It was quite one thing to dally with Berenice in Judea, but quite another in Rome. The elderly emperor probably could not fathom his son's passion for a foreign queen who was neither young nor beautiful nor able to bear children any longer. The Roman aristocracy was also displeased. Augustus's propagandizing that the victory of Cleopatra would mean the Orientalizing of Rome was still vivid in Roman minds. Senators almost certainly regarded Berenice as a second Cleopatra. Furthermore, the philosophers, most notably the Cynics, denounced the pair in the theater (Dio 66. 15. 4–5). Berenice's stay was further marred by a lawsuit. She was defended by the great rhetorician, Quintilian. In his magnificent treatise, *Institutio Oratoria*, he cryptically refers to some circumstances as similar to Cicero's in *pro Milone* (4. 1. 19–22). Unfortunately, he is silent about the facts of the case, although it may be speculated that he brought it to a successful conclusion. However, Berenice departed from Rome (Dio 66. 15. 4), perhaps hoping to return when the climate of public opinion was more favorable.

In 79, Vespasian died and Titus succeeded. Berenice was recalled and Titus appears to have been as much in love with her as ever. Suetonius remarked that his passion for Berenice was quite notorious (*Tit.* 7. 1). In spite of the fact that she was over fifty, she had retained his affection and probably believed that she would become empress. But again the Senate intervened. Titus had to choose between his beloved mistress and his throne. Like any sensible Roman, he chose his throne. *Dimisit inuitus inuitam*, "He sent her away, although neither desired this" (Suet. *Tit.* 7. 2).

Although Berenice had gambled for power and lost, she appears to have retired quietly. She probably returned to her brother's house in Judea. The fact that Titus died after a brief reign must have been small comfort. It may be guessed that she lived out the remainder of her life in peace, if not happiness.

The spread of imperial power beyond Italy in the days of the Republic created difficulties in the diplomatic dealings of Rome with the royal families of bordering kingdoms that gradually came under Roman influence or control. This situation was especially noteworthy in eastern areas with civilizations older than the Romans— thus Roman arrogance and royal pride came into conflict. The rulers of such client kingdoms were important in their own states, but they lacked independence since Roman military protection limited their sovereignty. Moreover, the Roman Senate and even Roman emperors never really accepted the idea of power exercised by royal women in their own right. Queen Cleopatra VII earlier and Queen Berenice in the Flavian period were beyond the bounds of the Roman social milieu.

V.

CALPURNIUS FABATUS

municeps morosus

The emperors filled the depleted ranks of the Senate with wealthy and able men from Rome, Italy, and the provinces. In the Republic before Augustus, there was a secondary aristocracy of wealth that took its name from an early military classification (*ordo equester*). In republican times, the equestrian class was chiefly concerned with business. Members bought contracts for government work including the farming of taxes, but beyond service in the army their only official function was service on the juries in the last century of the Republic. The most able or the most ambitious could and often did gain rank as senators.

Under the empire, the situation changed drastically, for Augustus and his successors selected members of this class to serve on many high official posts—financial as procurators, and administrative as prefects. These officials were appointed by the imperial chancery, received generous salaries, and served throughout the empire. They owed rank and appointment to the emperor and generally were more loyal supporters of the emperor than were the members of the Senate. A few such as Sejanus, praetorian prefect under Tiberius, or Cornelius Fuscus, praetorian prefect under Domitian, were notable. Most, however, are but briefly mentioned.

As time went on, more of these officials were drawn from Italy and the provinces. A good example is Pliny the Elder who died in the eruption of Vesuvius in A.D. 79

while commanding the imperial fleet. His literary work and the references in the letters of Pliny the Younger, his nephew and adopted son, determine his fame and success. Our knowledge of most of these men comes from the inscriptions, as in the example of Calpurnius Fabatus.

Fabatus, whose granddaughter was the third wife of the Younger Pliny, appears in Pliny's letters as a wealthy, cantankerous elder citizen. However, despite their familial connection, Pliny does not mention his early career of which we learn the details from an inscription set up in the Transpadane town of Comum (*ILS* 2721):

> Lucius Calpurnius Fabatus, son of Lucius, of the Oufentina tribe, a member of the board of six, of the board of four with judicial power, prefect of engineers, twice tribune of the twenty-first legion (surnamed) *Rapax*, prefect of the seventh Lusitanian cohort and of the six Gaetulian tribes in Numidia, priest of the deified Augustus, patron of the municipality, ordered in his will that this be set up.

This inscription is probably not a sepulchral one, but one for the base of a statue to be placed in a central location in his hometown.

Much information is contained in this formalized account. Fabatus's tribe is standard for Comum, his praenomen and his father's indicate free birth and Roman citizenship. His nomen might indicate a special grant of citizenship by a noble of republican times to an ancestor since universal citizenship in the Transpadane area was not granted until Julius Caesar was dictator. His cognomen might indicate an ancestor who was a good farmer since *fabae* ("beans") were not only a staple in the Roman diet but were also a most profitable crop.

The two earliest offices and the last two indicate

Calpurnius Fabatus

Fabatus's importance in Comum and also his wealth. The board of six is often mentioned in Comum, and appointment of youthful and wealthy men was both an honor and an obligation. This board was in charge of the local religious festivals and its members would be expected to defray the expenses of celebrations in honor of the gods and for the amusement of the poorer citizens. Early membership in the annual board of four was an even greater responsibility. These four men were the chief executive and judicial officers of a municipality, serving in a small way the functions of the consuls and praetors at Rome. They served without salary and either at the termination of their year in office or soon thereafter they were enrolled in the *ordo decurionum* ("municipal council") for life.

The last two offices came to Fabatus later in life. The priesthood involved only formal duties, but as patron of Comum he would represent the *municipium* at Rome, which implies a certain amount of oratorical and legal training. Moreover, this position would give him great authority in the municipal council and also a greater responsibility to be generous to Comum and its inhabitants.

The three offices listed in the center are of even greater importance in estimating his aim in life. The three are military in ascending, chronological order, and it is noteworthy that the third is of special significance. Thus, it is a safe assumption that he was successful in the first two. These offices prove what the rest of the inscription might imply, that he belonged to the secondary Roman nobility, the equestrian order.

The answer to Fabatus's abrupt abandonment of a promising career is to be found in a casual notice in Tacitus (*Ann.* 16. 8). In the year 65, Nero attacked L. Junius Silanus, whose father (as Nero) was the great-great-grandson (the Romans had a single word for this relationship—*abnepos*) of Augustus. Silanus (*atnepos*

Augusti), charged with incest by suborned informers and executed, was the last surviving male of the Julio-Claudian line except for the Emperor Nero, who survived him by only three years. The narrative of Tacitus continues :

> There were dragged in as accomplices the senators
> Volcacius Tullinus and Marcellus Cornelius and the
> Roman knight Calpurnius Fabatus. By appealing to
> the emperor, they avoided immediate condemnation,
> and soon, as men of less importance, they escaped
> Nero, who was intent on greater crimes.

Fabatus, about thirty at the time and with brilliant prospects, was then in Rome in 65, probably waiting for a procuratorial appointment. Due to misfortune there, he apparently withdrew discreetly to ancestral estates around Comum.

Since he had escaped condemnation, he had also escaped confiscation of his property that was extensive for a municipal knight, though no match for the property of many wealthy senators. In addition to the property in Comum, he had estates in Campania (Plin. *Ep*. 6. 30. 2) and in Umbrian Ameria (*Ep*. 8. 20. 3). No more would be known of him had not Pliny married his granddaughter about 104.

Pliny was apparently married three times, but the evidence, though disputable on points, yields this picture. His first wife is a shadowy figure and seems to have died young. She may have been from a wealthy Transpadane family. Roman marriages could be successful, but their arrangement among the upper classes stressed financial considerations rather than romance. His second wife came from a wealthy family, probably a senatorial family. She was the daughter of Pompeia Celerina (*Ep*. 1. 4) and died in 96 or 97 (9. 13. 4). After her death, Pliny remained on excellent terms with Pompeia who, either divorced or widowed, married Q.

Fulvius Gillo Bittius Proculus *frater Arvalis* and consul about 98.

The friendly relationship between Pompeia and Pliny is well illustrated by a letter about 100 in which Pliny is considering the purchase for three million sesterces of an estate adjoining his property near Trifernum in central Etruria (*Ep.* 3. 19). After noting that his resources are almost wholly in agricultural estates, he states : ". . . it will not be troublesome to borrow ; I will get it from my mother-in-law whose cash I use not other than my own" (8). However, his two references to his late wife's stepfather are quite hostile, for Proculus had spoken against Pliny in the Senate (*Ep.* 9. 13. 13) and the further reference in the same letter does not even use his name (23).

Perhaps Pliny had had enough of senatorial relatives since he turned in seeking a third wife to the family of Fabatus, who had married, probably after his return to the north in 65, and had a son and daughter. But Fabatus was not favored by fortune. By the turn of the century, he had long been a widower and had lost his son and daughter-in-law. His daughter, Calpurnia Hispulla, had earlier been on intimate terms with Pliny's mother : "You revered my mother in place of your mother" (*Ep.* 4. 19. 7). Hispulla had not married, which is surprising considering her father's wealth. She had raised her orphaned niece Calpurnia who at this time was a girl in her teens.

Pliny in his forties and now a consular senator chose wisely. To the Romans, the disparity in ages was not unusual. Calpurnia's dowry was large, and her husband was the most prominent man in Comum. The marriage was an extremely happy one and their mutual affection is reflected in the letters. The sedate senator began to write lyric poetry with more metrical skill than genius. The young wife memorized her husband's orations and set his poetry to music (*Ep.* 4. 19. 2–4). When Cal-

purnia had a miscarriage, Pliny wrote a touching letter
of mutual condolence to Hispulla (*Ep.* 8. 11). When
Pliny was appointed governor of Pontus and Bithynia,
Calpurnia accompanied him.

Pliny's love of his wife and his affection for her aunt
are clear, but his grandfather-in-law (Latin has a single
word for this connection—*prosocer*) must at times have
tried his patience. They had little in common and Fabatus apparently had a sharp tongue and once in a letter
apologized for his frankness. But Pliny was humane and
in good Roman fashion respected his elders. In answer to
Fabatus, he said: "From your letters I especially realize
how much you love me, since you deal with me as was
your custom with your own son" (*Ep.* 6. 12. 3). The last
two letters of the collection deal with Fabatus, Hispulla,
and Calpurnia. In 111, Fabatus died, and Pliny against
the rules gave his wife a passport to use the imperial
post for a rapid journey to Italy so that she might console her aunt. He explained this in a letter to the emperor
(10. 120) and received approval from Trajan in a
kindly and sympathetic fashion (10. 121).

Calpurnia disappears from the record. As a wealthy
widow in her early twenties, she probably remarried and
had the children denied to her and Pliny.

Fabatus's acerbity is not hard to understand, since
it most probably stemmed from rancor over his interrupted career and increased under the sorrow of repeated
bereavement. In his old age, his household must have
been upset by an unmarried daughter and a teenage
granddaughter. Of course, his bad temper could have
been pure personal malice.

VI.

SALVIUS LIBERALIS

frater Arvalis

After Vespasian consolidated his power in 69–70, one of his first tasks was to establish a policy that broadened the basis of the Senate and the equestrian class, which had been depleted by executions during Nero's reign and by the civil wars. Suetonius has this comment (*Vesp.* 9. 2):

> He cleansed the upper classes which had been drained by varying violent deaths and soiled by earlier negligence. He reviewed the Senate and the equestrians, removed the most unworthy and filled their ranks by choosing (*allecto*) the most honorable men from Italy and the provinces.

Two who rose to the consulship were L. Flavius Silva Nonius Bassus and C. Salvius Liberalis Nonius Bassus.

These two men were the notable citizens of *Urbs Salvia* (modern Urbisaglia), a municipality about a hundred miles northeast of Rome in the Picene area. This town, although wealthy because of its position in a fertile area, was almost unknown until the Flavian era when it became a *colonia*. It probably had been founded in late republican days. The emperors usually favored the wealthier families in such towns, and Silva and Liberalis were probably of equestrian rank and of wealthier families. The similarity of two of their names indicates some family ties—by adoption or by blood. They may have been cousins, or uterine brothers.

45

Information about Silva who was surely the elder comes solely from two recently discovered inscriptions and a reference in Josephus. He gained senatorial rank under Nero and commanded a legion in the civil wars. Soon after Vespasian arrived in Rome, he was chosen ex-praetor (*allectus inter praetorios*). This method of adding to the number of high-ranking senators (*allectio*) had been used by earlier emperors by virtue of censorial power. With the increase of both civil and military positions under the empire, for which a specific rank in the hierarchy of the Senate was a prerequisite, such a procedure could assure qualified officials. Vespasian used it more freely than his predecessors, and eighteen men are known to have been advanced by him in this manner.

In this case, Vespasian apparently needed a man of praetorian rank who was also experienced as a soldier, for Silva was appointed governor of Judea and commander of the legion stationed there. The capture and destruction of Jerusalem by Titus in 70 had not ended all resistance to the Roman arms. Silva's tenure from 73 to 80 included the siege and fall of Masada in 74 (Joseph. *BJ* 7. 252, 275–79, 304–407). From Josephus, we learn only that Silva was the Roman general. So eloquent had Eleazar, the commander at Masada, been that when the Romans entered, only two old women and five children had survived mass suicide. Even battle-hardened officers and soldiers must have been horrified.

Silva's reward from Titus, who had now succeeded his father, was the eponymous consulship for 81. It was probably at this time that he was inaugurated into the College of Pontiffs over which each reigning emperor presided as chief pontiff (*pontifex maximus*). There is no further information on Silva's senatorial career. Possibly Domitian derogated his administration of Judea. Perhaps he returned to *Urbs Salvia* and only occasionally visited Rome on official business as senator and priest. He was probably born not long before 40 and hence was too young to be excused from attending the senatorial meetings. Since he was patron of his native town and had twice been a high official there, he may have also come to Rome in the eighties on business for *Urbs Salvia*. The date of his death is unknown.

Of Salvius Liberalis, we have a much fuller account. He became a notable orator, and thus it can be assumed that early in life he left the Picene area to study with one of the leading teachers of oratory in Rome. He probably stayed with Silva, who about 62 held the first office leading to a senatorial career. Liberalis may have heard the great orator Domitius Afer in court, and he may even have attended him in his forensic activity as the notable teacher of rhetoric (rhetor) Quintilian did. He probably started a career in the courts as soon as Vespasian had established order in Rome.

We might suspect some rivalry between Silva, a *vir militaris*, and the younger man whose achievements were in the law courts, and in civilian administrative posts. The first specific reference probably falls in 71 or 72. Suetonius said of Vespasian that "he endured with the greatest lenience the epigrams of the lawyers" (*Vesp.* 13). The instance cited is that "he praised Salvius Liberalis who dared to say in defense of a rich defendant: 'What is it to Caesar, if Hipparchus has a hundred million sesterces?'" With a client so wealthy, Liberalis was doing quite well as a young advocate.

In 73–74, Vespasian and Titus held the censorship, and it was then that Silva was named to the patriciate, and Liberalis, probably on the recommendation of Silva, entered the Senate. The following inscription gives the details for this and for his further official career (*ILS* 1011):

To Gaius Salvius Liberalis Nonius Bassus, consul, proconsul of the province of Macedonia, judicial legate of the Augusti of Britain, legate of the fifth Macedonian legion, a member of the Arval Brethren,

enrolled by the deified Vespasian and the deified Titus
among the ex-tribunes, by the same emperors enrolled
among the ex-praetors, four times member of the
board of four with censorial powers, patron of the
colony. He when named proconsul of Asia declined
the office.

The double enrollment might mean that Titus reminded
his father that they were short of ex-praetors. Forth-
with Liberalis was dispatched to command a legion at
Oescus in Moesia. Perhaps the governor of Judea wrote
a letter full of military advice that Liberalis happily did
not need since the war with King Decebalus and his
Dacians occurred over a decade later.

After his return to Rome and his practice of law,
Liberalis was initiated into the Arval Brethren (*fratres
Arvales*) on 1 March 78. This religious association is of
the greatest significance for the history of Roman religion and for details on the events of the empire. This
priesthood was very old but had fallen into desuetude
until revived by Augustus. There were usually twelve
senators as members, including the emperor or in addition to him. Their chief duties were concerned with
ritual, especially presiding in mid-May at the festival of
the *Dea Dia* in a grove sacred to the goddess on the *via
Campana* about five miles from Rome. They also met at
Rome in the house of the chairman (*magister*) or in a
temple with vows for the safety and glory of the imperial
family and the empire.

Part of the ritual of this association included formal-
istic dance-steps by the priests, recitation of ritual
passages, and the chanting of a song so archaic that in
imperial times its meaning must have been almost incomprehensible to most of the priests and their attendants. As in many of the religious rites at Rome, the
Brethren also enjoyed elaborate banquets at which the
conversation, enhanced by the drinking of wine, turned

to such topics as the nature of the gods, the mortality of the soul, and the latest scandalous gossip.

Another part of the ritual was to record meticulously the minutes of each meeting (*acta fratrum Arvalium*), including the day of the month, the year by the names of the consuls, the business of the session, and frequently the names of the attending priests. These minutes were presumably recorded by the current chairman or, if he were absent, by an acting chairman (*promagister*), and they were so important that they were preserved on stone. Long passages and many minor fragments of these inscriptions have been recovered, some from Rome but most from the sacred grove of the *Dea Dia*. Complete or fragmentary minutes are preserved for twelve of the years of Liberalis's probable tenure. His presence is recorded in five of these years, and his absence in other years enables us to ascertain some approximate dates in his career.

The record for 1 March 78 marks the initiation of Liberalis as a priest (*ILS* 5027. 1–4; MW 8. 22–25):

> Under the same consuls on 1 March in the temple of Concord while the Arval Brethren were standing, in accordance with a petition of the Emperor Caesar Vespasian Augustus which had been transmitted to us we choose Gaius Salvius Liberalis Nonius Bassus into the place of Gaius Matidius Patruinus deceased.

After he gained the honor of this religious office from Vespasian, he was assigned by the same emperor to a task more suitable to his ability than the legionary command in Moesia. The post regularly held by a *praetorius* was that of a chief legal officer (*iuridicus*) and assistant to the consular governor of Britain. This post was held between May of 78 and 30 September 81, since at those two dates Liberalis was present at the sessions of the Arval Brethren. The consular legate of Britain was

Julius Agricola (consul 77) who probably arrived at his post at the beginning of the summer in 78. Liberalis may have joined Agricola as early as 78. Since the inscription cited above marks him as the appointee of two emperors (*legato Augustorum*), he was continued in his post by Titus, perhaps staying in Britain until the summer of 81.

The association of Vespasian, Liberalis, and Agricola with reference to Britain can arouse some historical retrospect and speculation. In earlier Roman times, this island was *ultima Thule* known only from the tales of Phoenician and Greek traders. Julius Caesar's two invasions brought more knowledge, but so puzzling was his purpose that the story was spread that he was hoping to obtain pearls there (Suet. *Iul.* 47). It is much more probable that he was training his legions in naval maneuvers in anticipation of action on the sea against Pompey in a civil war.

Pompey, Caesar, and Augustus had greatly expanded the empire, but basically the territorial additions were to protect the inner provinces. Augustus ignored the clamor of ardent patriots (for example, Horace *Odes* 1. 35. 29–32) to campaign beyond the Euphrates and in Britain and left a policy of no further expansion. Roman tradition of military glory was against such restraint, but the years from the death of Augustus in 14 to the assassination of Domitian in 96 saw only one violation of this principle, the attack on Britain.

Claudius attained imperial power without military experience or ability and chose Britain to buttress his rule. The adventure appealed to many Romans. Tacitus briefly mentions the expedition of Claudius (*Agr.* 13. 3):

> The deified Claudius was the author of so great a task, for he had legions and auxiliaries transported, and Vespasian was assigned for a part in this action. This was the beginning of good fortune soon to come to

Vespasian: nations were mastered, kings were
captured, and he was pointed out to the fates.

If these words were the only record of this invasion, the
historian could assume that the emperor was in personal
command and that Vespasian was his chief commander.
But the facts are far different as preserved elsewhere.

In 43, Aulus Plautius (consul in 29) was appointed
as imperial legate to Britain, and one of his legions,
the second Augustan, was commanded by Vespasian. In
44, the invasion had been so successful that Claudius
visited Britain, stayed sixteen days, and was present at
the fall of Colchester (*Camulodunum*). The emperor
then returned to Rome and celebrated a triumph for his
victories in Britain. His son born in 41 was now named
Britannicus. Thus, Claudius became a military hero.
Plautius and his subordinate Vespasian remained to do
battle until 47. Plautius was received at Rome with a
minor triumph (*ovatio*) since only members of the
imperial family were honored with a major triumph
(*iustus triumphus*), and Vespasian received the insignia
of a triumph (*ornamenta triumphalia*).

The early successes in Britain left many hostile areas,
and the revolt of Boudicca was quelled with difficulty by
Nero's legate Suetonius Paulinus. After the civil wars,
Vespasian, mindful of his service in Britain, had to
decide whether Britain should be abandoned or if the
conquest should be consolidated. Finally, he chose
Agricola as consular legate, presumably with instructions to bring the province into manageable form.
Flavian policy seems to have been against expansion and
despite absence of comment in the sources it seems unlikely that Vespasian anticipated the campaigns to the
north with which Agricola indulged himself. Moreover,
Vespasian may have had some reservations about his
new legate and as a consequence the appointment of
Liberalis may have been intended as a check upon the
governor.

With the accession of Titus, Agricola remained in Britain unwatched, since the new emperor had other interests. Within Titus's short reign, Liberalis returned to Rome, presumably delighted to be back in a civilized area. Surely his view of Agricola was far different from the laudatory account in Tacitus's biography, and it is easy to picture him as regaling his friends at banquets of the Arval Brethren with witticisms aimed at his staid superior in Britain. We may note that Tacitus never mentions Liberalis in *Agricola*.

With the accession of Domitian in 81, Liberalis's career flourished. In 81 and 86, Liberalis was present at meetings of the Brethren. In the interval, he was proconsul of Macedonia, which was then a senatorial province, without a legionary garrison, since the Danubian border was guarded by the forces in Moesia. His title was proconsul, as was true of the governors of all senatorial provinces even though these governors were *praetorii* except in Africa and Asia. An acephalous inscription that most probably is that of Liberalis's son C. Salvius Vitellianus lists the office of assistant (*legatus*) of the proconsul of Macedonia (*CIL* 9. 6365). It would not be unusual for a son to serve thus under his father.

A position as legate of an imperial province was a more certain preliminary to the consulship than that of a proconsul in a senatorial province. However, before 87 Liberalis held the suffect consulship. His career as a lawyer and as an administrator had probably gained him the favor of the young emperor who was much concerned with the courts and with good government in the provinces.

In this same period, Agricola was recalled from Britain, according to Tacitus because of Domitian's jealousy (*Agr.* 39). Again speculation can suggest an alternative view. Domitian had established a good military reputation by defeating the Chatti in 83 (Frontinus *Strat.* 2. 11. 7) and had celebrated a triumph and had received the cognomen Germanicus. He was then able to turn to the problem of Britain, and must have been appalled by the extent of Agricola's campaigns that proceeded much farther north than the emperor considered advisable. Moreover, Agricola's tenure in Britain had been unusually extended. Perhaps among the records he checked were Liberalis's reports as *iuridicus*. Then too he may have received derogatory information from his fellow *frater Arvalis* at one of their banquets. Most emperors ignored the meetings of the Brethren, but Domitian who took religion seriously attended frequently.

Some time during the next decade, he was on trial, (Plin. *Ep.* 3. 9. 33) for Pliny said that a notorious Spaniard Norbanus Licinianus (*Ep.* 3. 9. 33) was charged as if he had been "present with the prosecutors of Salvius Liberalis before a judge (*apud iudicem*)." This statement is in reference to the senatorial trial of the associates of Caecilius Classicus in 100 in Liberalis's presence. Pliny's comment is so brief that the date, the charge, and the outcome of the trial are unknown. It might be assumed from the context of the letter that the charge was treason (*de maiestate*), and that he had fallen out of favor with Domitian and was exiled. But the charge may have been less serious, and Domitian may have intervened for him. If this were true, Domitian may have been offended by the outspoken lawyer at a meeting of the Brethren—both were present when Liberalis presided as *promagister* early in 87 (MW 14. 1. 69–70). The young emperor lacked his father's sense of humor. Liberalis's absence from the meetings of the Brethren in 89–91 might indicate exile (MW 15–17), but the attendance at sessions was often sparse. Liberalis may never have left Rome except for frequent visits to *Urbs Salvia* with which he was always in close contact.

At all events, whatever the status of Liberalis in the last years of Domitian, he was surely in Rome not long after the accession of Nerva. The senators who had approved of Domitian, and Liberalis was probably one, had to be wary and most assented to the new ascendant anti-Domitianic furor that resulted in the cursing of the dead emperor's memory (*damnatio memoriae*). Not all, however, were against Domitian. Ti. Catius Caesius Fronto, one of the consuls in 96, made this ironic comment (Cary *Dio* 68. 1. 3) :

> When, now, no little commotion was occasioned by the fact that everybody was accusing everybody else, Fronto, the consul, is said to have remarked that it was bad to have an emperor under whom nobody was permitted to do anything, but worse to have one under whom everybody was permitted to do everything. . . .

When Tacitus published his biography of Agricola about 98, Agricola's former associate in Britain obtained a copy. Doubtless, it made an excellent conversation piece with many a witticism directed at the consular historian and his late father-in-law. Perhaps too Liberalis suggested that if Tacitus were going to write history, as had been rumored, he should learn to separate fiction from fact in his account of British campaigns. In the narrative of the revolt of Boudicca, Tacitus did improve, but Agricola's adventures appear in the lost books of the *Historiae,* and for these we must suspend judgment.

The first specific references to Liberalis later than 87 are in Pliny's letters and concern two senatorial trials in 100. In January, Pliny and Tacitus successfully prosecuted the Spanish-born Marius Priscus for maladministration as proconsul of Africa (*Ep.* 2. 11–12). Liberalis and a fellow *frater Arvalis* Catius Fronto, whose witticism at Nerva's expense is cited above, were the defense attorneys. Of Liberalis Pliny said : "On the next day Salvius Liberalis spoke for Marius, a man subtle with his material well-arranged, keen and eloquent : in this case he truly displayed his art" (2. 11. 17). Pliny's account makes it clear that Trajan who as the presiding eponymous consul favored the condemnation of Marius and probably disapproved of the attorneys for the defense.

Later in that year, Pliny prosecuted the associates of the deceased African-born Caecilius Classicus for misdeeds while Classicus was proconsul of Baetica (*Ep.* 3. 9). On the last day, Liberalis attacked the Spanish delegates for bad faith and by inference attacked Pliny who at this point called his opponent "vigorous and eloquent" (36). Obviously, there was no respect lost between Liberalis and Pliny, perhaps in part because of the younger man's well-documented hatred of Domitian and admiration of Trajan, perhaps in part also due to rivalry in the courts.

The summit of a senatorial career was a proconsular appointment to Asia or Africa, provinces restricted to senior ex-consuls, and assigned by lot (*sortitio*) to those who had held the consulship over a decade earlier. About this time, under Trajan Asia fell by lot to Liberalis, but he declined the appointment. It may have been because of his years since he was close to the age at which senators were excused from attending the senatorial meetings. Agricola in a similar situation declined such an appointment on the advice of Domitian, and Tacitus assigned it to the malignancy of the emperor (*Agr.* 42). Perhaps Trajan imitated Domitian here, and Liberalis may have regretted the violent passing of the *imperator damnatus*.

If Trajan may have been displeased with Liberalis, may not Liberalis have been displeased with Trajan? In 101, Trajan, *vir militaris*, in quest of glory disrupted peaceful relations with the Dacian king Decebalus and embarked on the First Dacian War. On 25 March 101,

Catius Fronto and Liberalis were present at a meeting of the Brethren held to offer special vows for Trajan in that war (Sm. 1. 22–73; *ILS* 5035):

> When Quintus Articuleius Paetus and Sextus Attius Suburanus were consuls on 25 March in the Capitolium, the Arval Brethren took these vows for the safety, return, and victory of the Emperor Caesar Nerva Trajan Augustus Germanicus in these words which are written below: "Jupiter the Best and Greatest, we pray, seek, and beseech you that you bring it about that the Emperor Caesar Nerva Trajan Augustus Germanicus, son of the deified Nerva, our chief and parent, chief pontiff, exercising the tribune's power, father of his country (we are of a mind to speak of him), return favorably and fortunately in good health and a victor from those areas and provinces which he will enter by land and by sea. And give to him a happy outcome of those deeds which he now performs or will perform, and preserve him in that good estate in which he now is, or in a better estate, and that you place him in Rome as soon as possible, brought back in health and a victor. But if you do this, in the name of the College of the Arval Brethren we vow to you sacrifice of a gilded bull. . . . There were present in the college Lucius Maecius Postumus, Lucius Julius Marinus Caecilius Simplex, Publius [*sic*] Salvius Liberalis Nonius Bassus, Tiberius Catius Caesius Fronto, Gaius Caecilius Strabo, Quintus Fulvius Gillo Bittius Proculus.

In the portion of the minutes omitted in my translation, there are recorded vows to Juno Regina, Minerva, Jupiter Victor, Salus *rei publicae populi Romani Quiritium*, Mars Victor, Victoria, Fortuna Redux, Vesta Mater, Neptunus Pater, and Hercules Victor.

The remaining years of Liberalis's life are not clearly dated and recorded in the ancient sources. It has been assumed that he was dead by 105 since he was absent from the meetings of 105 and 109 for which minutes are preserved. However, these minutes do not list the full twelve members and so are inconclusive. It is quite possible that he lived for some years after 101, and in those later years stayed in *Urbs Salvia*, enjoying his local prestige and visiting Rome only to represent his hometown or to further his son's career.

In concluding this account, we may return to the Picene town from which Silva and Liberalis came. Silva was twice chief official of the town, that is, a member of the board of four that exercised executive and judicial functions. In both instances, he was on that board when it also performed censorial duties, as it did every fifth year (*quattuorvir quinquennalis*). Once this position was held, these officers became the leading members of the town council and served for life. This local curia was to *Urbs Salvia* what the Senate was to Rome. In addition, Silva was *patronus coloniae*, in virtue of which honor he represented his hometown in Rome. He, his wife, and mother built an amphitheater for the town. All these items indicate familial wealth.

Liberalis was even more devoted to the town since he held a similar office four times, was likewise *patronus coloniae*, and a member of the curia. Even when he was a Roman official and engaged in an active legal career, he must have spent much time in his native town. He and his son, Vitellianus, built the structure where the council met, and in a year in which they were both on the board of four they added statues, columns, and donated money for the upkeep. These details are from a fragmentary inscription. Vitellianus held the same office as his father and served three terms.

We also know the name of Liberalis's wife from an epitaph raised by her son, for she survived her husband (*ILS* 1012) :

> To Vitellia Rufilla, daughter of Gaius, wife of Gaius Salvius Liberalis consul, priestess of the

Augustan Health, Gaius Salvius Vitellianus while alive (set this up) to the best of mothers.

Her priestly office was no small honor, since *Salus Augusta Salviensis* was the tutelary divinity of the town and the only temple known in the town was dedicated to this goddess. Father and son set up statues in the colonnades of the curia and there were probably three of them —those of Liberalis, Vitellia, and Vitellianus. Perhaps the inscription to the consul was on the basis of his statue.

When Liberalis died, surely the whole town participated in the obsequies, and the town council accompanied the grieving widow and her devoted son to the funeral pyre.

VII.

CORELLIUS RUFUS

consularis spectatissimus

The ancestors of Q. Corellius Rufus surely were of Cisalpine origin, undoubtedly wealthy, and of equestrian rank. Some of the Younger Pliny's references seem to imply Comum or a nearby Transpadane area.

Since Corellius committed suicide at the age of sixty-seven and since he probably died close to the time of Nerva's death, his dates may be set as about 30 or 31 to 97 or 98. No inscription outlines his career, and the first assignable date is about 78 for his consulship. This is late even for a *novus homo,* a man who rose from non-senatorial status to the consulship. Pliny, who was born in 62 or 63 was consul in 100. Probably Corellius's advance through the earlier offices was slow until he gained the favor of Vespasian and as a consequence obtained the praetorship and the consulate. It is also possible that he entered the Senate by the choice of the imperial censors in 73 when Vespasian and Titus filled the ranks by *allectio.* He would have been *adlectus inter praetorios* and eligible for the consulate, which is a less likely alternative since the men known to have been thus chosen did not gain the consulate so quickly. One possible reason for Flavian favor is that Minicius Justus, an equestrian and prefect of the camp of the seventh Galban legion was sent as an envoy to Vespasian late in 69 (Tac. *Hist.* 3. 7. 1). This man was the husband of Corellia, one of the sisters of Corellius.

Soon Corellius became imperial legate of Upper

Germany, probably from 79/80 to 82/83. This was a post of the greatest importance, held regularly by an ex-consul (*senator consularis*). The civil wars had shown clearly how important it was for the provinces heavily garrisoned by seasoned legions to be controlled by an able and loyal governor. *Upper* means up the Rhine and the legionary camps were close to Italy where no legions were stationed until over a century later.

The only proof of Corellius's position as commander of an extensive army is a bronze diploma of an auxiliary soldier discharged honorably (*ILS* 1995). Soldiers in the legions had to be Roman citizens, and so strict was the rule that a slave who had enlisted by falsely claiming such citizenship was executed (Trajan in Plin. *Ep.* 10. 30. 2). The auxiliary cohorts (foot) and wings (mounted) were recruited from free-born non-Romans. Their service was longer and their pay lower, but on discharge they received citizenship for themselves and for their children by one wife. These privileges were confirmed by an imperial law that was engraved on bronze and set up in Rome on the Capitoline or Palatine hills. This inscription contained the name of the emperor, the units and their commander, the legal provisions and the date, and the names of the individual soldiers. Such bronze tablets have all perished, but many copies made for the soldiers named have been preserved. These passports (*diplomata*) contain the provisions of the law on two small bronze plates, sealed with the names of seven citizens who certified the accuracy of the copy.

Such *diplomata* contain much information about the military history of the principate. This specific item reads in part:

> The Emperor Caesar Domitian . . . for those men who did military service on foot or in the cavalry in five cavalry troops and nine auxiliary companies of

infantry . . . and who are in Germany under Q.
Corellius Rufus.

The detachments named show that Corellius governed
Upper Germany. The document is dated 20 September
of 82 (or just possibly 83). The same law also lists
one troop and two companies from Moesia that had
presumably been detached for service to the northwest.
The date suggests that these auxiliaries were discharged
after Domitian's victory over the Chatti. Without doubt,
Corellius played a large part in this campaign on the
German border.

Since no source gives substantial evidence for any
position held by Corellius between 83 and 96, it has been
assumed that he did not remain in good standing under
Domitian, but one curious bit of numismatic evidence
and a casual reference in Pliny indicate that he also
did service in Asia. In the armed imperial provinces,
ex-praetors commanded one legion, ex-consuls more
than one legion, but all were called by the title "legate
of Augustus instead of a praetor" (*legatus Augusti pro
praetore*). In the senatorial provinces, the governors
were entitled proconsuls, but in all but Africa and Asia
they were ex-praetors. Appointments to these two consular senatorial provinces were the culminating honor
crowning a senatorial career even though military appointments such as Syria and the Germanies carried
heavier responsibilities.

Governors assigned to Asia and Africa were chosen
by lot from senior senators who held consulships twelve
to fifteen years earlier. Once Pliny harked back to a
legal problem that he had to deal with late in the reign
of Domitian and said: "I called into council Corellius
and Frontinus, two of the men whom our state had as
most outstanding (*spectatissimos*) at that time" (*Ep.*
5. 1. 5). The superlative *spectatissimos* applied to these
men seems to imply some similarity in careers.

Frontinus, in addition to being a notable writer on technical subjects, had a distinguished career. He was consul about 73, consular legate of Britain in 73/74–77/78 and of Lower Germany about 82/83–84/85, and finally proconsul of Asia in 86/87. Corellius, who was consul five years later than Frontinus, may have held a second consular post as imperial legate late in the eighties. The linking of the two men by Pliny might imply that both men were appointed to Asia in the middle nineties. The coins of Ephesus in which Domitian appears on the obverse and the Greek genitive of *Rufus* on the reverse enable us to interpret Pliny's reference. Rufus is a very common cognomen, but for these coins only Corellius Rufus is known to have had the qualifications for this proconsulship.

After the assassination of Domitian in September of 96, Nerva was announced the emperor, and Corellius became one of his advisers. He was probably a member of Nerva's council, although Pliny is not specific in his anecdote (*Ep.* 4. 17. 8) :

> When in the presence of the Emperor Nerva the conversation turned by chance on good young men, and the majority spoke of me with praise, Corellius contained himself in silence for a little while which added authority to him and then with that serious mien which you had ascertained he said: "I must praise Secundus rather sparingly because he does nothing except in accordance with my advice."

But in 97, Pliny, without consulting Corellius, during a Senate meeting charged that Publicius Certus was responsible for the execution of Helvidius Priscus in 93. Pliny much later in an account of that meeting naively informed his youthful protégé Ummidius Quadratus that for once he did not seek Corellius's advice since Corellius, being rather "hesitant and cautious" (*Ep.* 9. 13. 6), was sure to oppose such action.

Another example of Nerva's favor was his appointment to a senatorial commission that had a budget of sixty million sesterces to buy land and distribute it to needy Roman citizens (Plin. *Ep.* 7. 31. 4). Corellius's popularity with Nerva proved profitable to Pliny who had served as prefect of the military treasury under Domitian and was now appointed by Nerva to the more prestigious prefecture of the treasury of Saturn. These two prefectures were held by ex-praetors and the latter was usually followed by the consulship that Pliny held in 100.

The mutual devotion and admiration of these two men, who differed in age by thirty years, developed slowly. It had its inception even before Corellius went to Germany (*Ep.* 4. 17. 6). By the time Corellius had returned to Rome, Pliny had already appeared as an attorney in the courts in his eighteenth year (*Ep.* 5. 8. 8) and was already marked for senatorial rank, despite his equestrian origin, by his oratorical and financial ability. Corellius's advice and influence greatly helped the ambitious young man, but his constant recall of the older man and his continuing concern for the family of Corellius are sure indications that his devotion to him was based on a genuine and lasting affection.

Corellius had suffered from arthritic gout for over thirty years and in his latter days it became worse. About the time that Trajan succeeded Nerva, he decided to commit suicide by abstaining from food. Pliny's heartfelt tribute in a letter to his coeval friend, Calestrius Tiro, gives the details (*Ep.* 1. 12). Items from the letter picture his grief and that of Corellius's family: "I have sustained a most severe loss. Corellius Rufus has died, and of his own wish which aggravates my pain" (1). Pliny's grief was inconsolable (*insanabilis*), but he recognized the justice of Corellius's decision: "Indeed the best reason drove Corellius to this counsel, and for wise men reason is the equivalent of necessity"

63

(3). "In his thirtieth year, as I often heard him say, he was seized by pain in the feet" (4). But with resolute vigor he struggled against the pain until with increasing age the disease attacked all of his limbs. The idea of suicide was not new for Pliny continued: "I visited him during the time of Domitian as he was in bed in his suburban villa. . . . He looked round and said, 'Why do you think I endure such great pain so long? That I might survive that brigand even by one day'" (6–8). Both Corellius and Pliny, though favored by Domitian, were in that faction of the Senate that eventually opposed Domitian's open display of autocracy and his suppression of all plots against him except the last.

Pliny was not nearby when his elder friend first refused food. On the fourth day, Corellius's wife, Hispulla, sent a message through a mutual friend "that Corellius had decided to die and was not moved by her prayers or their daughter's; that I was the only one left by whom he could be recalled to life" (9). The old man's final word to such pleas was in Greek: "I have decided" (10). At the end Pliny said: "For I have lost, I have lost the witness, the guide, the teacher of my life" (12).

There is no evidence for Corellius's interest in philosophy or for his familiarity with Pliny's Stoic friends, but he was following the Stoic principle of approval of suicide when such an act was the result of rational considerations. Seneca discussed the problem of incurable disease as a reason for suicide and approved (*Ep.* 77). However, Corellius and Pliny were old-fashioned stoical Romans rather than professed Stoics.

In a later letter, Pliny recalls another statement by Corellius: "Indeed as he was dying he said to his daughter (she was accustomed to tell of this): 'In a rather long life I have gained many friends: nevertheless, Secundus and Cornutus especially'" (4. 17. 9). Cornutus was Pliny's colleague as consul in 100. Notably in this quotation the younger man was named first. Perhaps the thought back of these words was that his two friends would aid the surviving members of his family. At least in Pliny's case he was correct.

Corellius left as survivors "a daughter, wife, grandson, and sisters" (1. 12. 3). Presumably two sisters of whom one is not mentioned further by Pliny, but of the other he gives details in a letter of about 107 to Calpurnius Fabatus, grandfather of his wife (*Ep.* 7. 11). Corellia now in her old age had asked Pliny to sell her an estate in the region of the Lago di Como (*lacus Larius*). Pliny offered to sell her any of his estates except those inherited from his mother and father: "I am not able to yield these even to Corellia" (5). Apparently none suited her, but Pliny became heir to five-twelfths of a suitable estate and posted his part of the inheritance for sale. Before the auction, his freedman and agent Hermes was sent to Corellia and sold the land to her for 700,000 sesterces. The cross-grained Fabatus wrote to Pliny complaining that at auction the land would have brought 900,000 and implied that Pliny could repudiate the sale. The best interpretation of this letter is that he was protecting his granddaughter's rights. More probably he was merely giving vent to his bad temper. Fabatus may have disliked Corellia and her husband Justus, or there may have been some rancor due to his unsuccessful career in contrast to that of his granddaughter's consular husband. There is also a brief note to Corellia, confirming the authority of Hermes (*Ep.* 7. 14).

Pliny could have easily informed the elderly man that it was not his concern, but he patiently and politely explained his reasons. He said (*Ep.* 7. 11. 3–4):

> I cherish Corellia with the greatest reverence, first as the sister of Corellius Rufus, whose memory is sacred

to me, and then as the most intimate friend of my mother. I have old bonds with her husband Minicius Justus, a very fine man, and the greatest bond with their son, so great that when I was praetor he presided at the games I gave.

Justus was an equestrian, but his son was probably a senator thanks to the influence of his maternal uncle. He apparently did not outlive his parents.

Pliny has no further comment on Corellius's wife Hispulla, but twice he refers to the daughter Corellia Hispulla. The unusual names of mother and daughter may indicate connection with Comum and a familial tie with Pliny's third wife, Calpurnia, who was raised by her paternal aunt (*amita*), Calpurnia Hispulla, the daughter of Fabatus.

About 100 shortly after her father's death, Corellia Hispulla asked Pliny to recommend a Latin rhetor for her son Corellius Pansa (*consul ordinarius* in 122) who had completed his earlier studies with tutors at home. He was ready then for advanced instruction in oratory such as Pliny had had from the famous rhetor Quintilian (*Ep.* 2. 14. 9; 6. 6. 3). In a letter to Hispulla (*Ep.* 3. 3), he recommended Julius Genitor and said that he would be sponsor to Genitor's character.

The first section of the letter contains much information:

> I hesitate as to whether I looked up to your father, a most serious and righteous man, or loved him more, and I cherish you in memory of him and in honor to you. It is necessary that I desire and struggle in so far as I can that your son might be like his grandfather. I prefer indeed that he be like his maternal grandfather, although he has a paternal grandfather also notable and respected, his father and paternal uncle too are outstanding for distinguished praise.

In a letter written in 105, Pliny refers again to the daughter of Corellius (*Ep.* 4. 17). His own words are a fitting tribute to Corellius (4. 17. 4):

> The man is before my eyes than whom our age has produced no one more serious, more righteous, more subtle . . . I admired him more after I learned to know him intimately. . . . He kept nothing hidden from me, nothing humorous, nothing serious, nothing sad, nothing pleasant. I was very young, but from him I had honor and respect as from an equal in age. He was my sponsor and witness in seeking offices, my guide and comrade in starting tasks, my counsellor and ruler in carrying them out.

When Nerva became emperor, he surrounded himself with a group of elderly advisers, and Corellius was prominent in that coterie. Four of these older senators form an interesting contrast in their attitude concerning the *imperator damnatus*. Corellius was covertly hostile, at least in the latter years of Domitian's reign. Verginius Rufus, Pliny's guardian in his early days (*tutor*), was already *senex* when the last of the Flavians became emperor in 81, since he was born about A.D. 14. When he died in 97, Pliny wrote a long letter to Voconius Romanus recalling the memory of his aged friend. In this letter, Pliny noted that Verginius had lived under Domitian in retirement in his Etruscan estate, coming to Rome only when Pliny campaigned for and assumed his offices. Pliny added that he had outlived "Caesars to whom he was suspect because of his virtues" (*Ep.* 2. 1).

However, two of these men still favored the memory of Domitian: Fabricius Veiento and Sextus Julius Frontinus. The latter in his *Strategmata* four times referred favorably to Domitian in the war with the Chatti (1. 1. 8; 3. 10; 2. 3. 23; 11. 7). When the war in which Domitian commanded in person was successfully ended in the summer of 83, the emperor was styled Germanicus as a *cognomen ex uirtute*. Such an additional name for military valor was derogated after his assassination by his senatorial detractors (Tac. *Agr.* 39. 1 ; Plin. *Paneg.* 16. 3) as a sham victory. But Frontinus in his last reference wrote : "The Emperor Caesar Augustus Germanicus in the war in which he merited the cognomen of Germanicus—by conquering foreign enemies . . ." (2. 11. 7) and this still stood in his text after Domitian was killed.

The contrast between these two pairs of advisers under Nerva gives interesting insight into the continuity of imperial administration even when the imperial succession was marked by violence.

VIII.
DOMITIA
Domitiani uxor

History has not viewed Domitia Longina, Domitian's wife, kindly. In the sources, she does not appear as a congenial figure, for she was given a reputation nearly as bad as her husband's. But when examining the source materials more closely, we can see that she was not the deceitful and treacherous wife portrayed there.

Domitia came from a distinguished family. Her father, Domitius Corbulo, was Nero's most brilliant general, while her mother, Longina, may have been the daughter of the great jurist, Gaius Cassius Longinus. Domitia had an older sister whose name is not known. Corbulo was incautious in his choice of a husband for his older daughter, for he married her to Annius Vinicianus, who was closely allied to Piso and his conspirators. Apparently, Vinicianus wished to make Corbulo emperor. The plot was revealed (Suet. *Nero* 36. 1), and in 67 Corbulo was summoned by Nero to Greece and forestalled execution by committing suicide (Dio 62. 17. 5–6). Nothing further is known about this daughter, and it is possible that she did not survive her husband by many years.

Domitia was born 11 February, probably in the middle fifties. Her childhood must have been an exceptionally happy one. Her family's great wealth and influence could secure her the best Rome had to offer. Undoubtedly, she was carefully educated, moved in the best social circles, and could expect her father to arrange a good marriage for her. The scholiast on Juvenal writes that she was seduced as a child by the nobleman Rubrius Gallus (*ad Sat.* 4. 105). This story can be dismissed as mere gossip, for Corbulo's daughter probably was regarded as a great matrimonial prize and hence was strictly chaperoned. Furthermore, if Domitian had heard such a story, he refused to give it any validity. During his reign, Rubrius Gallus, who had campaigned successfully for Vespasian against the Sarmatians in Moesia (Joseph. *BJ* 7. 89–95), was honored with a place in Domitian's council (Juv. 4. 105–6).

Around 68 or 69, Domitia's family arranged for her to marry Lucius Aelius Lamia Plautius Aelianus. Lamia might have appeared to be a great catch, for he was the bluest of the blue bloods at Rome. He is believed to have been the grandson of the Lamia to whom Horace addressed an ode (3. 17). However, outside of his noble ancestors, Lamia had very little to recommend himself. He was probably more than twenty years Domitia's senior. This age difference in itself might not have been an obstacle to a happy marriage for one only has to witness the bond of genuine affection between the Younger Pliny and his youthful bride, Calpurnia (Plin. *Ep.* 4. 19; 6. 4; 7. 5). But Lamia was not Pliny. He had been married before and had a son. His prime interest was music (Suet. *Dom.* 10. 2), and his first wife may have been Appia, the music fanatic mentioned by Juvenal (6. 385–92). The anecdotes about Lamia indicate that he had a rather cavalier attitude toward marriage (Suet. *Dom.* 10. 2). He does not appear to have been a man of dynamic character, for so far as is known he never commanded an army or governed a province. Vespasian, who was always eager to recruit men of ability and good family into his service (Suet. *Vesp.* 9. 2), seems to have ignored him entirely. Juvenal may well have been thinking of Lamia when he wondered what value there was in family trees (8. 1).

It is not known how Domitian became acquainted with
Lamia and his young bride. Presumably, it was at
Rome. Lamia decided that his chance for advancement
could best be achieved through his wife. When Domitian
was fêted by Lamia, Domitia may have been ordered
to smile on young Caesar. Domitian was especially
vulnerable at this time, for he was a lonely young man,
hungry for affection and approval. His recent experience—the escape from the fire on the Capitoline, the
murder of his uncle by the partisans of Vitellius, the
disappointment of being denied a military command
(Tac. *Hist.* 3. 72–74; Suet. *Dom.* 1. 2; 2. 1–2)—must
have been traumatic to Domitian and must have increased his moodiness and sense of isolation. Still, it
would have been hard for him to resist Domitia. At
this age, she was surely beautiful as is evidenced by her
portraits on coins and the Capitoline bust that depicts her as an empress. Another bust in the Capitoline
labelled by Professor Hanfmann as "A Flavian Beauty"
receives from him this lyrical tribute (*Roman Art*
95):

> With her swanlike neck, feathery eyebrows, full
> lips, and fine aquiline nose, the unknown lady has
> poise and aristocratic bearing. If the paint of the eyes
> and on the lips had survived she . . . might have
> seemed more like flesh and blood. She inclines her
> head graciously rather than gracefully and her glance
> is cooly appraising. The artist had worked on the
> lively rhythm of that enormous enframing crown of
> hair, using the drill with virtuosity in the black and
> white accents of the corkscrew curls. The eyebrows
> are masterpieces of texturing.

This bust is from the Flavian period and was apparently
found together with a bust of Titus. She was labelled
"Giulia" (that is, Titus's daughter), but this identification is clearly wrong, for a comparison with the portraits
of Julia both marble and in the coinage indicates no

similarity. It is possible that this is a portrait of Domitia at the time she became Domitian's bride. The whole attitude fits a young aristocrat who has just married into the imperial family. There are similarities to her portrait as empress, and the differences could be explained by her greater maturity ten years later.

Yet it may not have been merely her beauty that attracted Domitian. Her erudition may have impressed him, for he was deeply interested in literature (Suet. *Dom.* 3). Furthermore, in these years she must have had a gentle disposition and a sympathetic ear, so that she was able to listen to Domitian and guess when he wanted her to say yes or no. Domitian was somewhat imperious by nature and it is highly unlikely that he would have been attracted to the domineering type of woman. Domitian fell deeply in love with her and soon he begged her to leave Lamia. He had found the melancholy world of Tibullus and Propertius oppressive, for he appears to have desired nothing more than to live openly with the woman he loved, to have a wife. At first Domitia seems to have hesitated, perhaps afraid that he would discard her once she left her husband. Yet when Domitian had made it clear that his intention was marriage, her choice was not difficult. It is unlikely that she had any respect left for the husband who had been willing to use her. Domitian, on the other hand, was young and handsome, devoted to her, and there was always the chance that he might be emperor one day. Lamia complaisantly agreed to a divorce, and in 70 Domitia married the youngest of the Flavians (Suet. *Dom.* 1. 3; Dio 66. 3. 4). It may be guessed that Vespasian was pleased that his son had found a bride of such beauty and of such good background.

Although the historians view Domitian negatively for taking another man's wife, divorce in imperial circles was a common thing. Octavian had taken Livia from Tiberius Claudius Nero when she was pregnant (Suet.

Aug. 62. 2). Gaius had taken Lollia Paulina and
Caesonia from their husbands (Suet. *Calig.* 25. 2–3),
while Nero's stealing of Poppaea from his boon companion, Otho, is luridly described in Tacitus's *Annales*
(13. 45–46). Usually, the husbands did not object.
Tiberius Claudius Nero calmly surrendered his wife to
Octavian when the triumvir indicated that he wished
to marry her (Suet. *Aug.* 69. 1). He even attended her
wedding (Dio 48. 44. 2–3). It was regarded as a stroke
of luck if the emperor cast his eye on the wife of another
man, for the husband who turned a blind eye might be
generously rewarded. Lamia does not appear to have
benefited materially from the divorce. It may be guessed
that Domitian, and probably Vespasian too, had only
contempt for a man who would use his wife so callously
for preferment. Titus made Lamia suffect consul in 80,
but he probably did so to insult his brother.

For the next ten years, Domitia and Domitian seemed
to have been happy. The sources do not hint at any domestic squabbles between them. Their niece, Julia,
probably came to live with them, for she could not go
to her mother and would need someone who could teach
her the ways of society and take her about as Phyllis, her
nurse, and Caenis, Vespasian's concubine, who were both
freedwomen, could not. During this time, Vespasian
awarded his younger son offices that involved more cere-
mony than actual work, so that he was able to spend a
great deal of leisure time with his family. In 73, the
much-desired son was born but died in infancy (Suet.
Dom. 3. 1). When Domitian became emperor, he immediately deified the child. On coins, Domitia appears
as Pietas, draped and veiled, stretching out her hands to
a child (*BMC* 2. 312, No. 65, Pl. 61. 9). On the reverse
of coins that bear her portrait, a naked infant, presumably *Divus Caesar* as the infant Jove, appears, seated on
a globe marked with cross zones, stretching out his hands
at his sides (*BMC* 2. 311, No. 61, Pl. 61. 6). Martial

wrote a touching epigram about how the deified son throws snow from the heavens upon his father who smiles at this action and in a later verse urged Silius Italicus to be brave over the loss of a son as Caesar was (4. 3; 9. 86). It would appear that the imperial couple had loved their little son very much and had never truly recovered from his death.

The accession of Titus in 79 cast a shadow over their lives. Titus appeared to have tampered with Vespasian's will that assigned Domitian a share of empire, as a result Domitian became bitter (Suet. *Dom.* 2. 3). Titus further exacerbated the situation by repeatedly requesting his brother to divorce Domitia and marry Julia. Domitian obstinately refused for he dearly loved Domitia (Suet. *Dom.* 22) and regarded the idea of marrying his niece with religious horror. The fact that Domitian declined to marry Julia when he might have done so legally would indicate that he did not harbor an incestuous passion for her. Julia remained on affectionate terms with her uncle to judge by the honors she received from him when he became emperor. Eventually Titus dropped the matter and married Julia to a cousin, Flavius Sabinus (Suet. *Dom.* 22), to whom she may have been originally betrothed. But he gave Domitian no peace, for he began making advances to Domitia, probably amused by the idea of taking his brother's wife. His own mistress, Queen Berenice, had been forced by public opinion to leave Rome (Suet. *Tit.* 7. 1–2). Domitia repulsed him, for she later swore a most holy oath that she had never committed adultery with Titus (ibid., 10. 2). This was one of the few charges that she had a chance to deny, and she should be taken at her word. Furthermore, it is extremely unlikely that Domitian, who was very religious, would have allowed her to perjure herself. If she had been guilty, it would have been more diplomatic to ignore the matter entirely. However, Titus's reign must have been a difficult period for

Domitia and her husband. His granting of the title
Augusta (*ILS* 266) to his daughter was an indication
that if Julia had had a son, he would have adopted the
boy. It may be guessed that there was a faction at court
that favored the idea of assassinating Domitian, and
another faction that supported him as Titus's heir. This
political tug-of-war must have put Domitian and his
wife under a terrible strain.

In 81, Titus died after a brief reign and Domitian
became emperor. Domitia was now the first lady in the
Roman Empire. Her husband was only too eager to
honor her, for she was hailed as *Augusta* (Suet. *Dom.*
3. 1). This title already appears as early as 1 October
81 in the *acta fratrum Arvalium* (MW 12, line 46). Her
birthday on 11 February and that of the emperor on 24
October were honored by an association devoted to the
god Silvanus (*collegium Silvani*) in Lucania (*ILS*
3546). Her name was included with that of her husband
in the vows offered by the Arval Brethren according to
the minutes extant for the years 81, 86, 87, 90, and 91
(MW 12–14, 16–17). Coins were issued in her honor
between 81 and 84 with her image on the obverse. On
the reverse of two coins there is an inscription *Concordia
Augusta* (*BMC* 2. 311, Nos. 60–61, Pl. 61. 4–5), on
the reverse of a third coin, she appears as *Fortuna
Augusta* (312, No. 64, Pl. 61. 8), and on a fourth coin,
she appears as *Venus Augusta* (353, No. 256, Pl. 68. 5).
Quintilian may have been thinking of Domitia as Pietas
when he wrote: "Certain ones must be praised because
their immortality comes by birthright, others because
they achieved it through virtue. The *pietas* of our prince
makes possible this glory of the present times" (3. 7. 9).
Furthermore, she was accorded divine honors in the East
at such centers as Brycus and Termessus (*IGRR* 3. 444;
4. 1152).

Yet Domitia's honors brought her little happiness.
The diadem of empire was not heavy on her head, for

as an aristocrat she saw her position as one to which she had been born. Domitia appears to have had no interest in influencing her husband's policies, and little else was required of her other than she be stately, proud, gracious, and perhaps a little kind. She must have discovered, once the novelty of her position had worn off, that she had gained an empire and lost her husband. The duties of imperial administration probably kept Domitian away from her much of the time.

Domitian himself at the day's end appears to have been weary of the crowds of people that constantly attended him, for he enjoyed wandering alone in a quiet part of the palace (Suet. *Dom.* 21). Domitia may have taken his desire for privacy as aloofness and bitterly resented it. The loneliness of her position made her miserable. Perhaps, to punish her husband for his neglect and to hurt him as deeply as possible, she turned to Paris, a matinee idol of the day. She may have believed that since she was empress, she could do as she pleased, and that she had a precedent. Messalina, Claudius's wife, had taken the actor, Mnester, as her lover. But Mnester had secured Claudius's consent (Dio 60. 22. 3–5), and Domitian was not Claudius. He had much of the puritan in him and did not relish being a cuckold.

His reaction was one of fury. He regarded Paris's conduct as the basest ingratitude, for the actor had been an imperial favorite (Juv. 7. 86–90). Paris was executed immediately, an action that was perfectly acceptable under the provisions of the Julian law concerning adultery. Dio says that he planned to put Domitia to death as well (67. 3). However, a man who has discovered that his wife is unfaithful is not about to be reasonable. At first, Domitian must have shouted that he would kill her, but when he calmed down he merely sent her away. There was surely no divorce as has often been assumed. According to Suetonius's biography, the ambiguous words *repudio* and *discidium* (3. 1), later *divortium* (10. 4; 13. 1), appear, but the basic meaning is "separation," and there is no hint of remarriage.

It has been alleged that in the meantime Domitian seduced Julia, and when he reconciled with Domitia through the services of a certain Ursus, he lived in a *ménage à trois* (Suet. *Dom.* 22; Dio 67. 3. 2). The allegation is unlikely. Julia did come to live at the palace about 84, for this was probably the time Domitian had found it necessary to execute her husband for conspiracy (Suet. *Dom.* 10. 4). Julia was his closest living relative, and he needed her support. He probably gave her Domitia's hastily vacated quarters which caused rumors that Julia had become his mistress. Julia may have reconciled Domitian and his wife, for she could speak bluntly to her uncle and tell him that much of the trouble was due to his neglect, while assuring him that Domitia was truly penitent and desired his forgiveness. Apparently he listened, for he did love Domitia. However, he was proud and possibly ashamed to admit he loved her in spite of all, so in an effort to save face, he recalled her on the grounds that the people had demanded it (Suet. *Dom.* 3. 1).

Their reconciliation was genuine. Domitian appears never to have brought up the matter again nor allowed anyone else to do so. Some years afterwards, the younger Helvidius Priscus wrote a farce, *Paris and Oenone,* that was supposed to have burlesqued the emperor's marital difficulties. Helvidius was said to have been put to death for his farce (Suet. *Dom.* 10. 4), but it seems more likely that the real charge was one of conspiracy. However, Domitia does not appear on coins at this time. Domitian, a deeply religious man (Suet. *Dom.* 4–5, 8; Dio 67. 9), may have felt that since Domitia committed adultery to have her represented as a goddess on coins was blasphemy. He did see that his wife had a more active social life. She presided at the games with him, and when she entered the amphitheater the crowd hailed her as *domina* (Suet. *Dom.* 13. 1).

She became interested in literature, for Josephus gratefully acknowledged the many favors he had received from her in his autobiography (*Vit.* 429), and Statius may have been a recipient as well. Time appears to have restored the imperial couple's original affection for one another, for Statius pictures them in his *Silvae* (93 or 94) as a happy couple whom Venus herself had joined in wedlock (3. 4. 53–54). It does not seem likely that Statius was being hypocritical, for if there had been domestic strife it would have been more convenient to ignore the matter entirely than to advertise what everyone would know to be false. Yet even though Domitian forgave his wife, the senatorial historians did not. Domitia went uncrowned forever in their minds for her single indiscretion.

Martial announces the impending birth of an heir in 90 in an epigram that appears to imitate Vergil's messianic eclogue (6. 3). The imperial couple must have been overjoyed at the prospect of a child. Nothing more is written of the expected child. It is unlikely that Martial was indulging in wishful thinking, for he was too cautious to appear to be drawing attention to the emperor's lack of issue. If a boy had died in infancy, Domitian certainly would have deified him. The silence might indicate a miscarriage or that a daughter was born.

The last years of Domitian's reign were not happy ones. Domitian was trying to reach an accord with the senatorial opposition but was repaid with continual conspiracies (Suet. *Dom.* 10; Dio 67. 11–13). Although Domitia may have found happiness in the care of a young daughter, in the faithful service of the youthful cupbearer, Earinus (Stat. *Silv.* 3. 4), and in the tempo-

rary adoption of her husband's great-nephews (Suet.
Dom. 15. 1), she must have constantly feared for her
husband's life. A portrait bust of her in the Capitoline
Museum probably belongs to this period in her life. It
shows a woman just entering middle age. Her features
are fuller and softer than those on the coin portraits of
the early eighties. There is a touch of melancholy that
is the most notable difference from the "Flavian Beauty"
which may well represent Domitia a quarter of a century
earlier. Perhaps the empress felt that she and Domitian
did not have much more time together.

The details of the conspiracy that left Domitian
bleeding on the floor are obscure. Cassius Dio's account is rather garbled. According to Dio, one of the
pages stole accusation tablets from under Domitian's
pillow as he slept. Domitia, who was ever in fear of her
life and an object of Domitian's hatred, found them and
gave them to the conspirators who hastened to complete
their plot (67. 15). The story is suspect. Why would
Domitian, who had an unenviable reputation for stealth
and cunning (Dio. 67. 1), hide documents of such importance under his pillow? He appears to have known
that a cabal was being formed against him (Suet. *Dom.*
16), and Domitia's finding the tablets may have been a
clumsy charade on his part to trap the guilty parties.
Furthermore, Domitia had no motive to become involved
in a conspiracy. There is not the slightest evidence to
prove that she and Domitian were on bad terms at the
time. If Domitian had really hated his wife as Dio suggests, he could have easily invoked the Julian law,
divorced her, and banished her to an island. Domitia
stood to lose all with the death of her husband. Since
she was a proud woman, it is highly unlikely that she
would desire to abdicate her position as empress. The
fact that she appears to have been absent from the palace
when Domitian was killed does not indicate complicity.

Shortly before his death, Domitian was afraid of an impending conspiracy (Suet. *Dom.* 16). Remembering the fate of Caesonia, Caligula's wife and stepsister of Domitia's father (Suet. *Calig.* 59), he may have sent her away to a safe place in case anything should happen to him.

Domitia lived on after 96, but there is no mention of this fact in Tacitus, Suetonius, and Pliny, although each must have known of her survival. Possibly Nerva protected her, aware of her rank and of her lack of influence in her husband's policies. With the stress on the anti-Domitianic policy under Trajan, senators would have been willing to connive with the "nonperson" status of the daughter of Corbulo and the widow of Domitian. One factor that may have protected her was the fact that Domitian had been favored by factions in the Senate and equestrian class, by many of the populace, and the army. There even may have been a feeling of guilt among those who hated Domitian.

Later writers never mention Domitia. Dio has a full notice of the death of Trajan's widow Plotina, but the circumstances of Domitia's life as a widow and of her death would be lost were it not for information supplied by inscriptions. They show that she did not live in poverty, that she retained the wealth inherited from her father, and that she may have retained some of the property given to her by Domitian.

Five inscriptions from Peltuinum name eight slaves or freed slaves of Domitia (*CIL* 9. 3418f., 3432, 3438, 3469). The first two are dedications to Silvanus, one by a freedman, one by a slave, and in the second she is listed as Domitia Augusta. The third is an honorary inscription (*titulus honorarius*) for two freedmen, both of whom were members of a board of six honoring the emperors (*seviri Augustales*), a priestly office granted to wealthy freedmen. Here too she is called Domitia Augusta. The fourth is a funerary inscription set up for a freeborn official of Peltuinum by his wife, Domitia Phoebe, freedwoman of Domitia. The last is also a funerary inscription raised by two men (slaves?) to their father who was "slave of Domitia, wife of Domitian."

Peltuinum was a *municipium* in central Italy on the borders of Pelignian and Sabine territory, about forty-five miles southeast of Reate, the birthplace of Vespasian. Clearly there was Flavian property in the town or near it, and this estate was certainly the gift of Vespasian or Domitian. The use of the title *Augusta* in two inscriptions and the inclusion of the name of the emperor in one may indicate a period before 96, but usage in inscriptions cited below may indicate the years after 96. Such an estate in the healthier area of Italy (Peltuinum is about twenty-five miles north of Sulmo, the birthplace of Ovid) would be an ideal summer retreat for an empress or a widow.

One singular facet of the Roman social structure casts light upon her later life. Most commercial operations were considered beneath the dignity of members of the senatorial class. The income necessary for members of the *ordo* was supposed to come from landed estates. The only respectable careers were in war, administration, and oratory. From prehistoric times, actual farming, or as wealth grew, the supervision of agricultural estates had been the basic occupation of the Romans. However, the manufacture of tile and bricks (*lateres*) was carried out on these estates and was viewed as a branch of farming. Until the time of Claudius, this was a small operation and the workshops (*officinae*) on the estates (*praedia*) were not of major importance since the chief product was roof-tiles. With a gradual change, especially in Rome, construction in which concrete was faced with brick became the norm. This usage was accelerated by the great fire of Nero's day. Hence the brickyards were expanded greatly. Since transport was expensive, and suitable clay was readily available, these *figlinae* expanded near the market for burnt brick. In Nero's days, the orator Domitius Afer invested in such estates, and eventually through his descendants the *figlinae Domitianae* formed the basis of the private wealth of Antoninus Pius and Marcus Aurelius. Such estates usually retained the name of the original entrepreneur.

Some time after 96, Domitia acquired estates containing the *figlinae Sulpicianae*. It is not known who the original owner Sulpicius was. It was the custom to stamp the bricks before firing; therefore, the following items would appear: the name of the *figlina*, the owner, the slave or freedman in charge of the *officina*, and at times a date by the names of the annual consuls. These first products of the *figlinae* were marked with stamps listing Domitia as the owner. On some of the 160 *lateres* listed by Dressel (*CIL* 15. 548–58) the consular dating falls in 123 and 126. Undated *lateres* might fall in the earlier or later period of that decade, but most likely somewhere within the middle. The distribution of the finds, where known, is at Ostia, in Rome, and on the *via Praenestina*, and provenience would indicate that the *praedia* were near Gabii, which is twelve miles east of Rome. The bricks could have been transported to Rome by cart, to Ostia by barge, and Gabii is on the *via Praenestina*. Thus Gabii, with a *villa suburbana* nearby was probably Domitia's residence in the middle years of Hadrian, and possibly throughout Trajan's reign. Far more interesting is the way in which Domitia is listed in the stamps, at times by abbreviation, but also by the full form *ex figlinis Domitiae Domitiani (uxor) Sulpicianis* ("from the Sulpician brickyards of Domitia, wife of Domitian"). Pliny is listed on inscriptions as *quaestor imperatoris* to avoid the phrase *quaestor Domitiani* and to avoid noting that he had been highly favored by Domitian (*CIL* 5. 5667; *ILS* 2927), but Domitia, ignoring the *damnatio memoriae* applied to her husband, boldly included his name on the widely spread product of her brickyards. Such action indicates her lasting love for her husband and her pride in having been his wife and his empress. The stamps also prove that Domitia did not marry again, even though many senators and knights would have been more than willing to wed the wealthy and still attractive widow of the emperor.

The date of Domitia's death is not certain. She was alive in 126 and died before 140. An inscribed marble tablet, found at Gabii, and now in Paris, gives the latter date (*ILS 272*) :

> In honor of the memory of the house of Domitia Augusta, daughter of Gnaeus Domitius Corbulo, Domitius Polycarpus and Europe, on a lot donated by a decree of the *ordo* of the *decuriones* (the town council of Gabii) built a temple (*aedem*) and decorated it with statues and other items with their own money and gave protection of the same (building) in perpetuity to the municipality (of Gabii) in accordance with the inscription written below.

In the second paragraph, a meeting of the council of Gabii is noted on 23 April 140 for consideration of a proposal to make the sacred building and a celebration connected with it the responsibility of the town. The third paragraph records the proposal before the town council :

> That Gnaeus Domitius Polycarpus in his own name and in that of his wife Domitia Europe offers to the *ordo* of the *decuriones* and of the *seviri Augustales* 10,000 sesterces. Already (*iampridem*) he had built a temple (*templum*) for the honor and memory of Domitia, daughter of Corbulo and adorns it with this mark of his devotion. . . . He turns to our enduring

town and asks . . . that the birthday and memory of
Domitia, daughter of Corbulo, be celebrated, and that
from the income of 10,000 sesterces distribution of
food be made to us as we recline in public.

The next two paragraphs record the acceptance by the
council of the money and the responsibilities entailed: a
final paragraph noted that "it was pleasing that this
decree be cut on a bronze tablet and posted in public
where it might clearly be properly read."

The formalized language of the inscription offers
speculation. In Cicero's day, Gabii had declined in importance (*Planc.* 23), but in Hadrian's day this and
other inscriptions indicate renewed prosperity, although
Juvenal used it, perhaps with some poetic license, as a
symbol of simple country life (3. 192; 6. 56; 7. 4; 10.
100f.). It is indeed possible that Domitia's presence gave
it added importance. If, as suggested above, her brickyards were in the vicinity of Gabii, some addition was
made to the prosperity of the town. It is clear that at the
date of the inscription it was a *municipium* with the
privileges of that type of town.

The names of Polycarpus and Europe indicate that
they had been freed by Domitia, since all of the slaves
she freed would normally take their *nomina* from her
father's name. Their *cognomina* come from their original servile names that indicate Greek ancestry. The
wealth of the couple makes it likely that Polycarpus had
been the chief official in her household, rewarded for his
services both while she was alive and in her will. Their
devotion to Domitia is a touching tribute to a kind and
loving *patrona*.

The word first used (*aedem*) might indicate a simple
shrine, but the second word (*templum*) marks a grander
structure. The original land had been granted by the
town council, and consequently the temple was certainly
within the area of the town itself. The bronze tablet

containing the official action was probably placed in the forum of Gabii, and the extant inscription was a marble tablet placed in the area of the temple. In the official language, she was given her title Augusta but was not listed as the wife of Domitian, as she listed herself on her brick stamps. Such listing was correct for she was widow, not wife. However, in dealing with the council Polycarpus may have been discreet since technically the *damnatio memoriae* had never been cancelled.

We cannot ascertain the date of her death since the temple had already been built in 140, and the word *iampridem* that was used is quite elastic. The best guess would place her death late in Hadrian's reign when Domitia was about eighty years old. Thus, she had out-lived Trajan and many of her harshest critics.

Again, there is no evidence to determine whose statues were erected in or in front of the temple. One is certain, that of Domitia. Did the inscription include the name of her husband? I suspect Polycarpus may have included Domitian's name, and he may even have defied the sena-torial decree and may have erected a statue of Domitian. He must have had the full confidence of his patroness and could have taken a risk that he knew would have pleased her.

In the years when Domitia was a widow, she probably spent much of her time in the suburban villa that, it may be assumed with great possibility, was near Gabii and, therefore, not far from Rome. She must have had many visitors who approved of the emperor despite the *damnatio memoriae*. She may also have maintained an establishment in Rome. Let us hope that she overcame bitter memories and lived through the remainder of her life resolute and imperious, but with calm fortitude as the years passed. Perhaps Hadrian was more kindly and allowed her ashes to be deposited in the *templum gentis Flaviae*.

The inferences drawn in the essay from the scanty

evidence concerning Domitia cast considerable light upon the character of her imperial husband. His widow's continuing devotion reveals much about his personality. The intimacy of marriage, even in the palace, would indicate traits of character that might not be obvious in public life.

IX.

FLAVIA JULIA

neptis imperatoris

Flavia Julia was the daughter of Titus and Marcia Furnilla. Her probable birth date was 63 or 64. Her parents' marriage was unsatisfactory, for Titus divorced his wife shortly after Julia's birth (Suet. *Tit.* 4. 3). Julia's mother, Marcia, may have been the niece of Barea Soranus, who perished in the aftermath of the Pisonian conspiracy (Tac. *Ann.* 16. 30–33), but the grounds for divorce were probably not political. Titus seems to have divorced his wife some time before the conspiracy of Piso. Possibly, he found Marcia dull, possibly she could not endure his passion for eunuchs and boys (Suet. *Tit.* 7. 1; Dio 67. 2. 3). It is unlikely that Julia ever knew her mother, for Roman divorce laws simply required the husband to return the dowry and to retain custody of the children, if he so desired.

Julia was entrusted to Phyllis, who had also been Domitian's nurse (Suet. *Dom.* 17. 3). Julia's affection for Domitian may have begun in early childhood. Domitian was certainly fond of his old nurse and must have visited her often. He may have helped to take care of his niece, coming to regard her as a younger sister, while she may have looked upon him as a brother or father. Titus's career allowed him neither the time nor affection for his daughter. He was quaestor in 67 and in the following year joined Vespasian in Judea where he eventually conquered Jerusalem (Suet. *Tit.* 4–5; Dio 66. 4–7). He may well have been disappointed that she was not a boy. However, when Domitian married in 70, Julia may have come to live with him and Domitia, for she would need someone who could teach her the ways of society and take her about as Phyllis or Caenis, both freedwomen, could not. If she stayed with her aunt and uncle, three years could have been happy ones for her.

In 79, Titus succeeded his father, and relations between him and his brother became quite strained, for Domitian suspected that Titus had tampered with Vespasian's will to deny him a share of empire (Suet. *Dom.* 2. 3). In the meantime, Julia had grown up and was now of marriageable age. The statue of her in the Braccio Nuovo of the Vatican Museum shows that she had become an ungainly, rather plump young woman, whose facial features bore an unfortunate resemblance to her father's and grandfather's. Titus maliciously offered Julia to Domitian with the understanding that he would divorce Domitia (Suet. *Dom.* 22). It is difficult to guess his motives. He may have desired to win Domitian over through family ties or perhaps acted on the suggestion of Berenice, as she had married her uncle, Herod of Chalcis. Domitian was horrified by his brother's proposition. He was devoted to Domitia (Suet. *Dom.* 22) and he must have recalled how the life of his favorite emperor, Tiberius, had been ruined when he was forced to divorce Vipsania to marry his wife's stepmother, the profligate Julia (Suet. *Tib.* 7. 2–3). Furthermore, he would remember the notorious marriage of Claudius and Agrippina. Although Claudius legalized marriages between uncles and nieces that were formerly looked upon as incest, only a freedman and a centurion cared to follow Claudius's example (Suet. *Clau.* 26. 3). Although Titus offered Julia repeatedly, Domitian remained adamant. Julia, too, may have been shocked at the suggestion and must have grieved at the strain that she was causing her aunt and uncle. Eventually Titus dropped his proposal and married her to a cousin, Flavius Sabinus, to whom she may have been originally betrothed (Suet. *Dom. 22*). Domitian's continued refusal seems to indicate that his affection for Julia was no more than the normal affection of an uncle toward his niece.

It was probably after the marriage to Sabinus that Julia was granted the title *Augusta*. The title appears in the minutes of the Arval Brethren for 3 January 81, when these priests offered vows (MW 11, lines 39–40): "For the health of the Emperor Titus . . . and Caesar Domitian . . . and Julia Augusta and their children." Antonia, the younger Agrippina, and Poppaea had each been either dowager empress or empress. The title was probably bestowed on Julia by Titus with the hope that she might quickly produce a male heir so that he might have a pretext to bypass Domitian as his successor. However, if this was Titus's intention, he was to be disappointed. Julia's marriage was childless and Titus died after a brief reign of two years.

During Titus's reign, Julia had been greatly honored. Besides receiving the title *Augusta*, she was identified with certain goddesses on coins issued in her honor. These included Salus, Venus, and Vesta (*BMC 2. 247*, Nos. 139, 141–42, 144, Pl. 47. 14–17), as well as Ceres and Concordia (ibid., 278–79, Nos. 253–58, Pl. 53. 5–6, 8). The choice of these deities is significant, for under the empire the emperor was regarded as the keeper of the *Salus* of the state, and since Julia was Titus's only child, the coin seems to indicate a desire for Julia's welfare. The identification with Venus is a common form of adulation that was frequently used in Rome and in Hellenistic kingdoms to honor the women of the royal houses. Julia as Vesta may refer to the possible granting of Vestal honors and privileges to her. Since Vesta was the guardian of the eternal flame and the eternity of Rome, this may indicate that Julia would guarantee through her issue the eternity of the Flavian dynasty. Ceres, of course, symbolizes the concern of the emperor for the grain supply of Rome and also for plenty. Finally, Concordia emphasizes the harmony within the imperial family, with the possible suggestion that affection within the imperial household makes possible concord in the empire.

Domitian, despite his rather acrimonious relations with Titus, appears to have retained his affection for Julia. She is called Julia Augusta in the inscriptions raised in her honor after the death of Titus (for example, *ILS* 266). Titus died on 13 September of 81, and on 1 October of that year the vows of the Arval Brethren were taken for the health of Domitian, Domitia, and Julia (MW 12). In 82, her husband was *consul ordinarius* as colleague of Domitian, then consul VIII. She is again linked with her uncle and aunt on the vows taken on 3 January 87 (MW 14). There may have been an agreement that if Domitian and his wife had no heir, the emperor would adopt any male children that Julia and Sabinus might have. However, Sabinus does not appear to have been content with his position. His ambitions seem to have gotten the better of him and probably in 83 or 84 Domitian found it necessary to execute him for treason (Suet. *Dom.* 10. 4).

At about the same time Domitian discovered that his wife was unfaithful. He must have been deeply chagrined, especially as he was trying to raise the morals of the populace (Suet. *Dom.* 8–9). In his fury, he dismissed Domitia and had her lover, the actor Paris, executed (Suet. *Dom.* 3. 1 ; Dio 67. 3. 1). Julia came to live at the palace, both to show her loyalty and to offer the support and comfort of her friendship that Domitian would have needed. She was probably given Domitia's hastily vacated quarters, which would explain the story that Domitian had divorced his wife and made Julia his mistress and consort. Suetonius states that Domitian loved her openly (*Dom.* 22), but surely there was no more than the normal affection between uncle and niece. It may have been Julia who reconciled Domitian and his wife, for as the emperor's friend and relative she could speak freely and offer advice without fear of incurring his displeasure. Domitian already missed his wife, for in spite of what had happened, he did love her. He relented and to save face issued a decree that recalled her because the people demanded it (Suet. *Dom.* 3. 1). Julia appears to have continued to stay with them, possibly as a companion for Domitia, more probably as an indication of their gratitude and affection.

This episode produced a curious side-story. According to Cassius Dio, Domitian and his wife were reconciled through the services of Ursus. Later Dio states that Domitian planned to kill Ursus, but at Julia's request made him consul (67. 3. 1; 4. 2). This story raises several questions. First, who was Ursus? He has been identified as Julius Servianus, who later became Hadrian's brother-in-law. It seems strange that Domitian would ask a comparatively unknown person to solve his domestic difficulties. Furthermore, what reason would Domitian have for wanting to kill him? The fact that Servianus became consul would indicate that the emperor regarded him favorably and wished to honor him. The story seems hopelessly tangled. A likely explanation is that Servianus's career was originally advanced through Julia's patronage. After the demise of the Flavian dynasty, it became fashionable for those who owed their careers to Domitian to ignore that fact. The wily Servianus may have invented the story of reconciling the emperor and his wife. Furthermore, since he had not been an opponent of the Flavian regime, he might have escaped the wrath of the anti-Domitianic faction by pretending that he had been in danger too. It is unlikely that anyone would wish to contradict him, especially since the denigration of Domitian was officially sanctioned. By Hadrian's time, there would be few people left who could recall the actual circumstances.

Julia died in the period 87–89, since her name is not added to those of Domitian and Domitia in the vows of the Arval Brethren on 3 January 90 (MW 16). Her early death gave rise to an extremely ugly rumor. Pliny (*Ep.* 4. 11. 6), Juvenal (2. 29–33), and Suetonius (*Dom.* 22) state that Domitian had made her pregnant and had forced her to undergo an abortion that caused her early death. None of these writers is reliable on this point. Pliny was only too willing to repeat something that made Domitian appear cruel and lustful in contrast to Trajan. Juvenal's hatred of Domitian bordered on obsession, for Domitian may have exiled him. Furthermore, he exaggerates the story, for he pictures Julia terminating several pregnancies. Suetonius repeats the story of the abortion, but he does not confirm it.

The story is difficult to believe for several reasons. Even if Julia had conceived her uncle's child, is it likely that the emperor who so greatly desired a son and heir would force her to abort it? Domitian had persistently refused Julia's hand in marriage years before, and his action would seem to indicate that he did not have the slightest desire, even when he might do so legally, of entering into a relationship that he regarded as incestuous. Furthermore, Julia is not called promiscuous by the sources. It is possible that she may not have been pregnant at all. Julia may well have suffered from an ovarian tumor producing the appearance of pregnancy and eventually killing her, thus the reason for the story of the pregnancy and abortion. Domitia does not appear to have believed the tale, for years after her husband's death, in spite of the *damnatio memoriae* applied to his name, she boldly signed as Domitian's wife on many inscriptions (*CIL* 15. 548–58). She would hardly have done so if she had not loved him or had believed him to have been guilty of such an act.

Domitian must have been grief stricken at Julia's death, for he had lost one of his truest friends. No doubt, the rumors concerning the fatal abortion caused him considerable pain. He soon deified Julia. Her consecration is celebrated on a gem in the British Museum that depicts a bust of Julia carried aloft by a peacock, the bird which carried women who were deified to the heavens, just as the eagle carried men. Furthermore, Julia was honored as *Diva Iulia* in 90–91 on the reverse of coins of Domitian (*BMC* 2. 403–4, Nos. 458–63, Pl. 80. 3). Cult centers arose in the west at Aeclanum in the Samnite area not far from Naples (*ILS* 6487), at Novaria in Transpadane Italy east of Milan (*CIL* 5. 6514), at Celeia in the procuratorial province of Noricum (*ILS* 8906). When Domitian and his wife were expecting a child in 90, Martial heralding the birth stated that Julia herself would spin a golden life-thread for the heir (6. 3. 5–6). Nothing more is said about the expected child that might indicate a miscarriage or that the expected son and heir turned out to be a girl who may have been named after her cousin.

During her lifetime, Julia must have been distressed that she had caused her uncle so much trouble through no fault of her own. She would have been pleased if she had known of the service that she would do for Domitian in death. After Domitian was killed, Phyllis, their faithful nurse, and a few retainers stole his body away and cremated it in her gardens before an angry Senate and populace could take their revenge on the body of the dead emperor as they had with Sejanus and Vitellius. Phyllis carried Domitian's ashes to the Flavian temple and mixed them with Julia's so that they might rest undisturbed (Suet. *Dom.* 17. 3). Undoubtedly, Domitia both approved and respected Phyllis's beau geste.

X.

AQUILIUS REGULUS

delator et orator

The epigrams of Martial, and the writings of Tacitus and Pliny, offer insight into the character and oratorical ability of Marcus Aquilius Regulus. The poet is favorable, but the verdict of the other two is hostile. Scholars are inclined to discount Martial, and accept the denigration of Regulus. Sir Ronald Syme in his *Tacitus* (1. 102), while noting his oratorical excellence, admitted that Regulus was guilty of histrionic affectation and moral obliquity. Betty Radice was even harsher, for she states in the introduction to her Loeb translation of Pliny's works (xvii) : "The one person he cannot tolerate is M. Aquilius Regulus whose flamboyant affectations and unscrupulous ambitions are the exact antithesis of Pliny's solid principles and unaffectedness." However, there is ambiguity in the sources, and the estimate of Regulus is subject to some revision.

The year of his birth is uncertain. However, while quite young, he undertook several prosecutions successfully and gained the quaestorship under Nero (Tac. *Hist.* 4. 42. 5) about 66 or 67. Since the minimum age for the quaestorship was usually twenty-five, a birth date of 40/41 would be likely.

Practically nothing is known of his early life. His parents must have been divorced some years after his birth, for his mother remarried, a Vipstanus, probably L. Vipstanus Poplicola Messalla, who was consul in

48. From this union was born Vipstanus Messalla, who was to loom large in Tacitus's *Dialogus*.

Since his father was wealthy, Regulus received a good education. It is possible that he studied with the famous grammarian Palaemon. Once he had mastered the fundamentals of oratory, he may have trained himself the old-fashioned way, attending court and observing the various speakers, noting both their good and bad points. There was a series to choose from: Domitius Afer, the Younger Seneca, Vibius Crispus, Silius Italicus, and Servilius Nonianus.

Before 65, his father appears to have had financial difficulties and had gone into exile. A charge of treason can be discounted, for had there been such Tacitus would surely have mentioned it. The estate was confiscated and divided among creditors, leaving the young Regulus poor and without prospects (Tac. *Hist.* 4. 42; Plin. *Ep.* 2. 20. 13). If he wished to retrieve fortune and station, he had but one choice, to exercise his oratorical skill.

His first prosecution was that of the elderly consular Ser. Cornelius Orfitus. Both Suetonius and Dio state that Orfitus was condemned in 66 for owning three shops near the forum (Suet. *Nero* 37. 1; Dio 62. 27. 1). The charge is trivial. Possibly Orfitus was using the shops for treasonable purposes, such as meeting places for a conspiracy. The Pisonian conspiracy had been crushed the year before, and consequently Nero was suspicious that a number of senators harbored treasonable intentions.

M. Licinius Crassus Frugi, the brother of the Piso who was adopted by Galba, was next, but the charge is not known. In 67, Regulus successfully prosecuted Q. Sulpicius Camerinus, Piso's father-in-law, and his young son. The ostensible charge was possessing the cognomen *Pythicus*. Yet it was not Regulus who initiated their downfall, for Dio specifically states that Helius, who had been left as prefect of the city while Nero was in Greece, was responsible (62. 18. 2). It can be assumed that the freedman discovered some evidence and asked Regulus, a staunch supporter of the regime, to take the case. The zeal with which Regulus undertook the prosecution of those connected with the family of Piso and the fierce hatred toward them that was to span twenty-five years (Tac. *Hist.* 4. 42; Plin. *Ep.* 2. 20. 2) suggest that they might have been involved in the ruin of his father.

That Nero appreciated his efforts is clearly shown by the honors he bestowed upon him: the quaestorship, seven million sesterces, and a priesthood. Regulus's zeal in tracking down individual senators who were suspected of treason and in encouraging autocratic behavior toward the Senate suited Nero's mood (Tac. *Hist.* 4. 42).

If Regulus had hopes for a long and profitable career under Nero, he was soon to be disappointed. His activities after Nero's fall are unknown, but the anecdote of his biting Piso's severed head (Tac. *Hist.* 4. 42) would indicate that he had bitterly opposed the adoption of Piso and may well have been one of those who supported Otho. Nothing is heard of him until 70 when the Flavians had secured imperial power. In the early months of 70, the Senate was vainly trying to revive its moribund authority by demanding vengeance on informers, especially three, Sariolenus Voculus, Nonius Attianus, and Cestius Severus (Tac. *Hist.* 4. 41). Then Regulus's head was demanded, for the wife and children of Crassus were calling for his blood. Vipstanus Messalla, Regulus's half-brother, interceded for him. Although Messalla was not old enough to hold office, he had friends of sufficient influence (Tac. *Hist.* 4. 42). Messalla had been a military tribune in the Flavian army (Tac. *Hist.* 3. 9. 3, 18. 2), and perhaps he had secured

the appointment through Regulus's influence. The fact
that he was willing to face an angry Senate on behalf of
Regulus would indicate feelings of fraternal affection
and gratitude.

Curtius Montanus answered Messalla bitterly, accus-
ing Regulus of giving money to the murderer of Piso
and even of biting the dead man's head, a story that
Tacitus clearly regarded as false, for he did not even
consider it worth mentioning when he described Piso's
death (*Hist.* 1. 43–44). Montanus felt that Regulus
had no reason to become a delator because his youth and
poverty protected him from Nero's envious eye, that he
had become one through sheer lust for blood and greed
for gain. Yet Montanus never states that Regulus's victims were innocent of charges, as if their rank alone
absolved them. In short, he condemns Regulus for not
wanting to be poor, for having talent and ambition, and
most of all, for supporting the emperor.

Tacitus surely intended the reader to assume the worst
of Regulus, but a peculiarity in his method of composition is significant. The really serious charges are not
stated as categorical facts but are included in the speech
of Montanus that Tacitus presumably found recorded
in the minutes of the Senate (*acta senatus*). An interesting inverted parallel can be found in the *Annals* (13.
42–43). In A.D. 58, Publius Suillius, a noted senator
and prominent as delator under Claudius, was tried by
the Senate for receiving remuneration for pleading
cases. In his own defense he attacked Seneca (42. 2–4).
The charges made by Suillius against Nero's adviser
are belied by the historian in other passages. Thus in
neither of these two cases did the historian prove the
accuracy of the charges made in speeches delivered in the
Senate.

Regulus's rescue was eventually effected by Domitian
and Mucianus, who favored amnesty (Tac. *Hist.* 4. 44).
He must have realized how dangerous the situation had

been, for he was never again involved in a prosecution for treason. Since he was already wealthy and had a reputation for eloquence, he no longer needed such risky pursuits. Nothing is heard of him for the next fifteen years, except for a fleeting reference in Tacitus's *Dialogus*. Marcus Aper chides Vipstanus Messalla for his antiquarian tastes and declares: "For I have often heard this speech of yours, when forgetting your own eloquence as well as your brother's, you argue that no one of your own day has the right to the title of orator" (*Dial.* 15. 1). This statement indicates that Regulus's practice was flourishing.

As an orator, Regulus appears to have left nothing to chance, patching his right eye if he was prosecuting, his left if defending, consulting the omens, and using all the time that was allotted to an attorney (Plin. *Ep.* 6. 2. 2, 5). It is difficult to gauge his style. His quips about Pliny's Stoic friend Rusticus indicate an extremely sharp tongue (Plin. *Ep.* 1. 5. 2), and the epigrams that Martial addressed to him show that he was not lacking in humor (7. 16, 31). Pliny described him as eloquent (*Ep.* 1. 5. 2) but also said that he had weak lungs, stuttered and stammered, took untold ages to find the right word, and had no memory whatsoever, although he did concede that Regulus possessed a perverse sort of genius which coupled with bold impudence had compelled him to become an orator (*Ep.* 4. 7. 4). Probably Regulus varied his delivery: quick and witty when the occasion called for it; slow and unabashedly simple when there was need to emphasize key points.

Regulus does not seem to have held further offices after 70. It might justly be asked how a man of such outstanding talents could have been kept from the praetorship and consulship, since being a delator was not a permanent stain on one's career. Yet the Flavians may have decided that Regulus, though effective in the courts, did not have the steadiness to command a legion or to administer a province. Domitian does not seem to have liked him and turned to others for legal aid such as Pegasus, Vibius Crispus, Catullus Messalinus, Fabricius Veiento (Juv. 4. 76–83, 113–29). Yet Regulus himself may not have desired a political career and may have been quite content to put money in his purse and to be king of the courts. If there was going to be a consul in the family, let it be Vipstanus. However, after his appearance in the *Dialogus*, the dramatic date of which is believed to be 74/75, Vipstanus Messalla disappears from history. No public document or transaction of the Flavian age bears his name. Messalla would have been quaestor about 74, and his aristocratic connections should have carried him to the consulship a decade later. It is reasonable to conclude that Messalla died before he was of the proper age to stand for higher office.

Martial and Pliny, however, bring Regulus into the light of history once more. His relationship with Martial will be examined first. In 85/86, the Spaniard had published his first book of epigrams that contains three pieces about Regulus. The first two are about a portico at the orator's Tiburtine villa that collapsed after a visit (1. 12, 82). Martial remarks that fortune dared not brave the odium of killing him and adds that Regulus is under the care of the gods as the ruin harmed him not. Again he states that Regulus's wisdom and piety are no less than his genius, so that one could not help but offer him incense (1. 111).

Martial was flattering Regulus for a specific purpose. This book was his first ambitious publication and he wanted people to notice. Domitian received several epigrams on the subject of hares and lions that can only be described as effusive, and they more than hinted at the emperor's divine power (1. 6, 14, 22, 104). Regulus, as an important man, received his share of flattery. Martial was not looking for presents, but for prospective patrons.

Regulus appears to have noticed, but not to the extent that Martial wished. The epigrams addressed to Regulus in the succeeding books contain a couple of mild jokes and in pieces written to others, Regulus's name is used merely as a byword for eloquence (2. 74, 93; 4. 16; 5. 10, 21, 28, 63).

In the sixth book published in 90, the tone changes and reveals a much warmer relationship. There is a charming picture of family life centering around Regulus's little son. It would appear that Regulus married in middle age. His wife may have been Caepia Procula (*CIL* 15. 7421), possibly the daughter or sister of Caepio Hispo (Plin. *Ep.* 4. 9. 16). Martial pictures the boy, not yet three, sitting on his mother's lap, then leaving it to hear his father declaim. The poet prays that Regulus will live to hear his son plead and that his wife may hear them both (6. 38). Martial may have been thinking of the passage in the *Iliad* when Hector prays that his son will grow up to be a great warrior and come home to place the spoils that he has won at his mother's feet, so men will declare that he is a much greater man than his father (6. 466–81). However, Martial goes further. Unlike Astyanax, who cried and tried to crawl away, frightened by his father's helmet, little Regulus crawls to his father upon hearing his voice. Regulus, the greatest warrior of the courts, so Martial hopes, will live to see his son perform.

The other epigram in the book is less personal. A poet of low birth had insulted Martial. In defense, Martial lists all the important people who approve of him, including Regulus (6. 64. 11).

The seventh book published in 92 further confirms a close friendship. It contains two jokes. In the first, Martial quips "I have no money at home, so only one remedy remains, Regulus. I must put your gifts on the auction block. What do you bid?" (7. 16). Later Martial sends Regulus a gift of expensive farm produce, but it is not from his estates; Martial bought it at the market (7. 31). Such are the jokes one can make to a good friend. It can be guessed that the friendship between Martial and Regulus was based on mutual admiration. Martial felt no desire to don the gown and plead, while Regulus does not seem to have taken refuge in the hills of Helicon after a hard day in court. It is to Martial that we owe our knowledge of Regulus's primacy in the courts in this period, for had Regulus not been the acknowledged king, Martial would have used some other orator as a byword for eloquence.

In the remainder of the books, Regulus is not mentioned. There are probably several reasons. The eighth book is primarily concerned with Domitian. The stormy political scene after Domitian's death was a difficult time for both of them. Martial was not one to swim against the current and returned to Spain.

Regulus's relations with Pliny were considerably less cordial. Pliny had made a successful debut in court at the age of eighteen and had won fame (*Ep.* 1. 18. 3–5; 5. 8. 8). Regulus's early relations with Pliny seem to be rather patronizing. He appears to have disapproved of the younger man's predilection to cover every point in a case, no matter how small. He probably felt that this detracted from the case and made the delivery loose and disjointed. His own statement, "I go for the jugular" (*Ep.* 1. 20. 14), describes his own style: find the main points and ply them for all they are worth. He also disapproved of what he considered to be excessive use of Cicero as a model by Pliny (*Ep.* 1. 5. 11). May not Regulus have felt that no one could touch the great orator of the Republic, and that Pliny, able as he was, was trying too hard and should concentrate on the eloquence of his own times?

About 93, when Pliny prosecuted Baebius Massa and his Stoic friends were disgraced, his relations with Regulus took an abrupt turn for the worse. We may speculate that this happened for political, personal, and professional reasons. Regulus may have been deeply hurt and insulted that he was not chosen to prosecute Massa. In all likelihood, Domitian wanted a prosecutor who owed his advancement to the Flavians and who would be a fitting representative for the regime. Pliny was the ideal choice. If there was professional jealousy, two things exacerbated the situation. Regulus was fiercely hostile to the Stoic circle that included many of Pliny's friends: Arulenus Rusticus, Herennius Senecio, Junius Mauricus, Mettius Modestus, Arria, and Fannia. He appears to have disliked Rusticus the most, for he called him a Stoic ape and added that he was branded with the mark of Vitellius (*Ep.* 1. 5. 2). Apparently he regarded Rusticus as a mere poseur and a man who, in spite of all his high principles, would serve a creature like Vitellius. It was with the heartiest satisfaction that he saw Rusticus condemned in 93 (*Ep.* 1. 5. 2). Why he disliked Senecio is less clear. He may have bitterly resented Senecio's remark about him to the effect that as an orator he was an evil man skilled in speaking (*Ep.* 4. 7. 5). Mettius Modestus had won his implacable hatred by writing to Domitian that Regulus was the vilest of all two-legged creatures (*Ep.* 1. 5, 14).

But what incensed Pliny particularly was Regulus's attempt to trap him into a treasonable statement. The two were on opposite sides of a case in 92/93. Pliny defended Arionilla at Rusticus's request, an act that must have intensified feelings on both sides. The case hinged on a point made by the jurist Mettius Modestus who was then in exile. Suddenly Regulus asked: "I ask you, Pliny, what do you think of Modestus?" Pliny was taken aback, for to answer favorably would invite a treason charge but to answer otherwise would make him appear the most craven of men. Again the same question. Pliny refused to answer unless the court demanded it. Regulus tried a new approach and asked: "What do you think of Modestus' piety?" Pliny was able to escape the trap, but he never forgave Regulus for putting him in such danger ,(*Ep.* 1. 5. 5–7). Pliny was never specific about why Regulus acted so meanly. Mere professional jealousy does not explain it. Although Regulus bitterly hated Modestus (*Ep.* 1. 5. 13–14), this was not sufficient cause to attack Pliny.

Once Domitian was dead, Regulus was naturally fearful in the confusion that followed. He had been in danger twenty-five years before and there was no Vipstanus to stand by him this time. Rightly fearing Pliny's plans to prosecute him, he begged such distinguished men as Caecilius Celer, Fabius Justus, and Vestricius Spurinna to reconcile him to Pliny, but Pliny was adamant (*Ep.* 1. 5. 8–14). He refused to make any decision until the return of Junius Mauricus, Rusticus's brother, from exile. He wrote to Voconius Romanus that Regulus would be hard to prosecute because he was wealthy and influential, but the attempt might be successful, for he noted that the goodwill the wicked have is as unreliable as themselves. However, he would wait until Mauricus returned and seek his advice. (*Ep.* 1. 5. 15–16). In the end, he dropped his plans for prosecution. Mauricus may have advised him to do so, for Pliny did not have a strong case. Regulus had not been a delator during the Flavian regime, and while he despised Rusticus and his friends hatred was a flimsy charge.

Regulus is not mentioned during Nerva's reign except for an odd anecdote in the *Epitome de Caesaribus*. A certain Regulus is said to have caused the emperor's death after an altercation with him (12. 10). The story is a puzzling one, since it is highly unlikely that Regulus would risk his already shaky position by arguing with the emperor. It is quite possible that Nerva may have criticized Regulus's conduct under Nero and the Flavians, and Regulus may have responded in turn with a bold account of Nerva's part in quelling the Pisonian conspiracy (Tac. *Ann.* 15. 72).

Regulus weathered this political storm too, and returned to his law practice. In the second book of Pliny's letters, he is present at the trial of Marius Priscus, urging a consular senator, Pompeius Collega, to propose a resolution that he himself did not follow, an act that was sharply criticized by Pliny (*Ep.* 2. 11. 22). The fact that he did not propose the motion might be a further indication that he was only a senator of quaestorian rank, for had he been of praetorian or consular rank he surely would have been given a hearing.

A second letter sheds an ugly light on his character. Pliny eagerly recounts the amazing adventures of Regulus, the legacy hunter (*Ep.* 2. 20). Yet Regulus may not have been so greedy for legacies as Pliny believed, for he gives only three examples, each of which deserves to be examined individually.

Verania was the widow of Galba's adopted son Piso. Pliny states that she and Regulus were on the worst possible terms. Their mutual hatred must have spanned nearly three decades. When Verania was ill, he came to see her, asked her the day and hour of her birth, and made calculations. He informed her that she was going through a period of danger but would survive it, and he would consult a soothsayer to make certain if this was so. He performed a sacrifice at once and declared the entrails favorable. Verania, out of mistaken gratitude, changed her will and left him a legacy. Not long afterwards, her illness grew worse and she died, cursing Regulus (*Ep.* 2. 20. 2–5). Yet Regulus may have tricked her into giving him a legacy, not because he was so eager for her fortune but as an ironic jest, to have the last word in their feud.

Velleius Blaesus was a consular senator about whom nothing definite is known. Regulus had hoped for a legacy from him but did not receive one (*Ep. 2. 20. 7–8*). Regulus may have been Blaesus's attorney and may have expected some return for his services. His eagerness for Blaesus to die and Blaesus's cutting him off suggest that there was little amity on either side.

The case of Aurelia is quite open. She desired to make a will and called witnesses, among them Regulus. He asked her to leave him the costly garments that she was wearing. At first, she thought that he was joking, but she gave in and even satisfied him by letting him read her will (*Ep. 2. 20. 10–11*). The fact that Regulus was a witness indicates that he was a trusted friend. Furthermore, if he could make such a request and have it granted, there is a strong probability that he was Aurelia's lawyer. Indeed, Aurelia's sole objection may have been his asking for such a trifle.

Pliny's case falls apart. It is likely that Regulus sought legacies for professional reasons, but not from greed. It is common knowledge that Roman law forbade lawyers' fees. The legal way to pay a successful attorney was to leave him a legacy. Cicero is the prime example of a lawyer who gained wealth this way (*Phil. 2. 16*). Regulus, as the premier lawyer, naturally expected some gratitude from his clients and may have been somewhat exacting, a trait traceable to the poverty of his youth. But Pliny's picture of a millionaire lawyer going out of his way to bait the rich and childless is ridiculous and would have fooled no prospective victims unless they were in their dotage.

After Trajan became emperor, Regulus and Pliny appear to have made peace and may even have appeared on cases together (*Ep. 6. 2. 3*). But if Regulus's career flourished, his private life was not going smoothly. First his wife died. And like a great many men who become fathers late in life, he spoiled his adored son shamelessly. He freed him from parental authority so that the lad might inherit his mother's fortune. It was more probably a desire for the boy to enjoy himself that led Regulus to do this, rather than to keep some kind of hold over his son through excessive kindness or to inherit from his son as Pliny so maliciously asserts. As for the boy himself, Pliny admits that he was a promising lad and was amazed that he did not turn out far worse (*Ep.* 4. 2. 1–2).

The boy died suddenly about 104. Regulus, an emotional person, grieved bitterly (*Ep.* 4. 2. 3). Pliny, usually so sympathetic when it came to the deaths of friends, relatives, and children (*Ep.* 5. 16; 8. 23; 10. 120), takes a perverse pleasure in Regulus's misfortune. He goes so far as to say that Regulus's grief was a sham and that now he will be the target of legacy hunters as he deserves (*Ep.* 4. 2. 5). It is doubtful that the childless Pliny could understand his rival's loss. Later when the bereaved father wrote a life of his son, Pliny gleefully remarked that it was written by a boy rather than about one, and lamented about what wonders Regulus could have done had he been a good man (*Ep.* 4. 7. 3, 7). His hatred of Regulus made it impossible for him to use any restraint. Yet it was hardly Regulus's fault if he lacked Pliny's personality and ambitions.

The unhappy Regulus did not survive his son by many years. Pliny wrote to his friend, Arrianus, about 106, that he missed Regulus in the courts, although he was quick to add that he did not wish him back. However, he admitted that Regulus was a man who honored oratory, although he meanly noted that he was never able to memorize his speeches (*Ep.* 6. 2. 1–3). Faint praise for the late king of the courts.

It is not known for certain what the reputation of Regulus's speeches was in the centuries that followed, but there is one tantalizing bit of information. Martianus Capella, a fifth-century rhetorician, in the fifth book of his voluminous work entitled *de nuptiis Philologiae et Mercurii* listed in chronological order the men whom he considered to be the great Roman orators, with the exception of Cicero. These included the Gracchi, Regulus, Pliny, and Fronto (5. 432). Both Pliny and Fronto might reasonably claim this honor on the basis of their extensive literary works. Yet Regulus, who does not seem to have published much, is linked with these two notable authors. The passage hints that Regulus's orations were still extant and that he was honored by rhetors and orators alike because he had honored oratory.

Regulus was apparently a man without great political ambition, content to be a senator of low rank, and quite willing to cast his lot with each reigning emperor. He had qualities that did not appeal to Pliny, and as Pliny tended to overpraise his friends, so he over-vilified this rival orator of whom he disapproved. The basic reason was hatred of the *delatores*.

In the early empire, these prosecutors were scorned by many whose friends or relatives suffered death or exile on conviction of treason. However, since there was no public prosecutor, *delatio* in all periods was a legal necessity. Such a system is subject to abuse, but in many prosecutions the basic charge was introduced by frivolous charges to set the tone. These less weighty charges are at times the only ones preserved in the sources, and consequently it is often difficult to be certain of the guilt or innocence of the defendants when they were on trial for treason against the emperor (*de maiestate imperatoris laesa*).

XI.

CORNUTUS TERTULLUS

senator orientalis

A notable feature of the spread of Roman power in Italy in the early Republic is the generosity of grants of full or partial Roman citizenship. This was a key factor in the ability of the Roman Senate to maintain its military forces and morale in the years when Hannibal was ravaging Italy. Later this policy was gradually restricted until the Social War of 90–88 B.C. broke out. The aim of the Latin allies in this war was the extension of citizenship, and Rome won the war by granting most of these demands. Under the dictator Caesar, this grant was extended even to the Transpadane section of Cisalpine Gaul that now became part of Italy. In addition, senatorial generals had granted citizenship to many prominent men in the provinces, whose pro-Roman sympathies had aided conquest and administration. Most of these men were wealthy since Rome was timocratic and favored the upper, conservative classes.

In Italy a myriad slaves were added to the citizen body by manumission. Caesar's generosity in granting citizenship after he defeated Pompey and the Senate in the civil war was somewhat restricted by Augustus and Tiberius. Claudius was more generous and so too were the Flavians. The process continued apace until under Caracalla an edict of A.D. 212, the *constitutio Antoniniana*, granted citizenship to all free men in the empire.

Caesar claimed that he descended from Jupiter and

King Ancus Martius, but Pompeius Magnus was from Picenum that was not conquered by Rome until early in the third century B.C. The influence of the expansion of *civitas Romana* was even greater on the cultural level. Cicero came from the Volscian town of Arpinum, and the Volsci were not absorbed into the Roman state until the third century. In that same century, the first figure in the development of Latin literature was Livius Andronicus, a freed Greek slave. Maecenas, the minister of Augustus and the patron of literature, was descended from Etruscan kings, and Vergil was from Transpadane Mantua.

The Roman Republic was not only timocratic but also aristocratic. The balance of royal, aristocratic, and democratic powers, as outlined by Polybius and Cicero, was not a real balance, since the aristocratic Senate dominated the government until a few notable senators with military backing shattered the republican system and created an empire. As might be expected, recruitment of new Senate members was far less extensive than into the citizen body. Birth and place of origin played an important role. In the early Republic, military ability and origin in and around Rome was essential for new members of the Senate. In the later Republic, in addition to military ability, origin in peninsular Italy and oratorical fame aided some men to gain senatorial status.

In the last generation of the Republic, Cicero was almost unique as *novus homo*, a man born into a non-senatorial family who became a plebeian noble by gaining the consulship. Sergius Catilina, a patrician noble, could bitterly call him in a senatorial exchange (Sall. *Cat.* 31. 8) *inquilinus civis urbis Romae* ("a foreign-born citizen of the city of Rome"). A few chance references indicate senators born outside of Italy; for example Q. Caecilius, who contested with Cicero the right to prosecute Verres in 70 B.C., had been Verres's quaestor and was a Sicilian by birth. Lucius Cornelius Balbus, born in Spanish Gades, had great influence at this time, but it was only in 40 B.C. during the civil wars that he attained the consulship.

The change came slowly with the emperors. There are a few examples under Augustus and the Julio-Claudian emperors, although more data might increase the numbers. Provincial senators first came from the western provinces—an example is Valerius Asiaticus, born in Vienna (modern Vienne) in Gallia Narbonensis, who, consul in A.D. 35 and a second time in 46, fell under Claudius on suspicion of treason the year after his second consulship.

When Claudius in 48 proposed granting the right to stand for offices that gave senatorial rank to *primores Galliae* ("chief men of Gaul"), some members of his imperial council bitterly objected (Tac. *Ann.* 11. 23). Was it not enough that the Insubres and Veneti (peoples of the Transpadane area) had this right without extending it to tribes that had fought against the deified Julius? Of course, the emperor overrode such objections, since the council was advisory only.

Under the Flavian dynasty that, though Italian with its origin in Reate, was more sympathetic to the provinces, the procedure flourished. The examples from literature are few, but the inscriptional evidence adds significantly to the known provincial senators, especially those from the eastern provinces. The Flavian policy was carried on and accelerated under their successors until in the days of Marcus Aurelius there was a considerable portion of the Senate drawn from the Orient.

In general, such men from the provinces were able soldiers and administrators from whom the emperors expected efficient and loyal support. To be sure, such choices could not always be a success. Two examples of eastern senators who gained senatorial rank under the Flavians form an interesting contrast. Q. Pompeius

Falco, consul in 108, whose family almost certainly came from the Lycian-Pamphylian area of Asia Minor, held consular posts of the greatest importance in Italy and the provinces. In contrast the career of Cornutus Tertullus, suffect consul with Pliny in September and October of 100, was not a success.

As might be expected, Pliny makes a number of references to his colleague. Two are highly complimentary but the rest are rather casual. Indeed Pliny's picture of his colleague is vague and ambiguous. So much more can be added from an inscription outlining the whole of Cornutus's career that we are warned against trusting Pliny as a wholly reliable source.

Before 100, it is clear that Cornutus was well known to many of Pliny's friends. Corellius Rufus had noted that his two most intimate friends were Pliny and Cornutus (*Ep.* 4. 17. 9), and Cornutus was connected in some way with a group of Pliny's Stoic friends who suffered under Domitian in 93. They were probably involved in treasonable activity, for Senecio, Rusticus, and Helvidius were executed while Mauricus, Gratilla, Arria, and Fannia were exiled. Pliny adds that he too was in danger (*Ep.* 3. 11. 3), although in 94 Pliny was appointed by Domitian as prefect of the military treasury, a post that he was still holding in 96.

Early in the reign of Nerva, Pliny attacked Publicius Certus in the Senate and threatened prosecution for his role in the execution of Helvidius (*Ep.* 9. 13). Actually Nerva intervened and no prosecution followed. But in the discussion, Cornutus, as legal guardian of Helvidius's daughter, spoke for the family (9. 13. 16). In 98, Pliny and Cornutus shared appointments as prefects of the treasury of Saturn (*Ep.* 5. 14. 5), which they held until their joint consulship.

In January of 100, Pliny and Tacitus prosecuted Marius Priscus for criminal activity as proconsul of Africa (*Ep.* 2. 11–12). Trajan, as one of the eponymous consuls of the year, presided and it is clear that he favored a harsh verdict. When motions were called for, Cornutus, as designate suffect consul, gave his *sententia* early and favored such a harsh penalty for Priscus that some senators, loath to penalize one of their own members, favored greater lenience, but the motion of Cornutus passed (2. 11. 19–22). Thus he pleased Trajan and Pliny. Pliny called him "an excellent man and very steadfast for the truth," perhaps induced to the compliment because Cornutus "added at the end of his motion that, because Tacitus and I had performed the prosecution assigned to us diligently and bravely, the Senate judged that we had acted in a manner worthy of the role assigned to us" (2. 11. 19). In the case of a subordinate of Priscus, Cornutus also made a motion for a harsh penalty, but it was defeated (2. 12. 2).

When the two men became consuls on 1 September, Pliny delivered a speech of thanks (*actio gratiarum*) to Trajan in the Senate. Since he spoke for both, we may assume that Cornutus was not an accomplished orator. These speeches that were customary were presumably quite short, but Pliny later revised, amplified, and published the *Panegyricus*. The theme was the contrast between an evil Domitian and a virtuous Trajan. As was fitting on such a formal occasion, he spoke highly of his colleague. Here too Pliny spoke of the events of 93: "The despoiler and executioner of each best man had breathed on both of us by the slaughter of friends . . ." (*Pan.* 90. 5). If Pliny did not fall into direct danger with Domitian, we may assume that Cornutus was also safe.

The next reference to Cornutus in the correspondence is about 105. Pliny had just been appointed as curator of the bed and banks of the Tiber and the sewers of the city (for the title compare *ILS* 2927) and then learned that Cornutus had been designated curator of the Aemilian road. In a letter to a mutual friend, Pliny wrote of his colleague in the highest terms (*Ep.* 5. 14. 2–5):

> I am not able to express with what joy I am affected
> in his name . . . because, though he be as he is, far
> removed from all ambition, nevertheless a pleasing
> office has been given to him. . . . However what is
> better than Cornutus, what more righteous, what
> more clearly exhibited with all praise as an example
> of early days? This is known to me, not by his
> reputation which he enjoys best and most deserved,
> but by extensive and great experience. Together we
> love and have loved almost all of both sexes whom
> our time has brought forth to be emulated. This bond
> of friendships bound us with closest familiarity. There
> is added the bond of shared public duty. . . . I followed
> him as a teacher, revered him as a parent.

At first glance, this encomium implies an intimate friendship such as that which Pliny enjoyed with Corellius Rufus. However, other references to Cornutus do not confirm such closeness. Several reasons for this fulsome praise may be adduced. Pliny, as he himself admitted, tended to overpraise those people of whom he approved (*Ep.* 7. 28). Moreover collegiality in office was always a bond in Rome. The passage suggests two other possibilities. The stress on mutual friends makes it inherently possible that the recipient of the letter was on more familiar terms with Cornutus than Pliny was. Also Pliny shows the good Roman virtue of respect for his elders.

In the seventh book, the only letters addressed to Cornutus appear. Neither tells us much of the recipient. The first is a brief note of thirteen lines thanking Cornutus for his concern over the eyestrain Pliny was suffering, and for the gift of a fat hen—an odd present for a gentleman farmer (*Ep.* 7. 21). The second recommends Pollio, an equestrian friend, to Cornutus (*Ep.* 7. 31). There is much about Pollio, including a connection with Corellius Rufus, but no hint as to the reason Pollio wishes to become a friend of Cornutus. Perhaps there was some business deal in the offing.

In summary, this is the picture of Cornutus in Pliny, a man of talent and good character. He was older than Pliny but was less dynamic and aggressive. Probably he was not an orator, and there is no indication that he was an attorney. He and Pliny had mutual friends in the senatorial aristocracy, among them senators opposed to Domitian. Pliny implies strongly that his career was retarded by Domitian, and then flourished under Nerva and Trajan. Pliny gives us no hint of his origin and background, but it could be inferred from his comments that Cornutus was most probably Italian.

A fuller and rather different picture emerges from the funerary inscription (*titulus sepulcralis*) that, pre-served only by copies, was originally inscribed on a huge altar at Tusculum (*ILS* 1024):

> To Gaius Julius Plancius Varus Cornutus Tertullus, son of Publius, of the Horatian tribe, consul, proconsul of the province of Africa, proconsul of the province of (Gallia) Narbonensis, propraetorian legate of the deified Trajan Parthicus of Pontus and Bithynia, propraetorian legate of the same (emperor) of the province of Aquitania for holding the census, curator of the Aemilian road, prefect of the treasury of Saturn, propraetorian legate (of the proconsul) of the province of Crete and Cyrene, enrolled among the ex-praetors by the deified Vespasian and the deified Titus as censors, Cerealian aedile, urban quaestor. Gaius Julius Plancius Varus Cornutus (set up this funerary monument) in accordance with his will.

The third and fourth of Cornutus's six names are con-jectural but surely correct. *Africae* is now certain rather than the earlier conjecture *Asiae*. The heir who set up the inscription is an obvious relative and probably his

son. Inscriptions from Perge on the coast of Pamphylia
in southern Asia Minor mark the eastern origin of
Cornutus. The wealth and importance of this family
is clear.

Since the normal age for the praetorship was thirty,
Cornutus's enrollment *inter praetorios* by Vespasian and
Titus as censors in 73 would set his birth date about 43.
Hence he was about twenty years older than his consular
colleague. Cornutus was certainly a *novus homo* who
stepped into the senatorial order by election to the quaestorship. It is surprising that he did not hold the military and civilian offices that often preceded a senatorial
career. It is unlikely that they would be omitted in this
type of inscription. In inscriptions listing a senatorial
career, the offices are usually listed in ascending or descending order. The latter is used here.

The dates for his various early offices are not certain,
but he was probably quaestor under Nero, and aedile
about the time Vespasian assumed power. He may have
come to the new emperor's attention because of his
eastern origin. His *adlectio* is unusual. Of the eighteen
men known to have been advanced under Vespasian,
Cornutus as ex-aedile was the highest in rank and consequently profited but little by the action of the imperial
censors. He was probably assigned immediately as legate
(assistant) of the proconsul of Crete and Cyrene. Such
an assignment usually went to a *praetorius*, but at times
to lower-ranked senators. His eastern origin may have
been the reason for the choice of province, but there is
no evidence in the inscription that he was much concerned with relatives in Perge.

His position as proconsul of Narbonensis was probably under Vespasian, perhaps 78–79. Although this was
an important post, it did not lead to the consulship so
surely as did military appointments such as commander
of a legion and an appointment to an imperial province.
Its position in the inscription is unusual. The consul-

ship and a major priesthood would stand first out of order, but a proconsulship in a senatorial province would be in normal order.

From about 79 to 97, Cornutus held no office. This could be explained by his friendship with men hostile to Domitian, but Pliny was friendly with the same group and was highly favored by Domitian. An alternative view is not only possible but also highly probable. Ninety years ago the great Theodor Mommsen called Domitian "one of the most careful administrators who held the imperial office." I suspect that Domitian inspected the record of Cornutus and decided that he did not meet the high standard of efficiency that the young emperor deemed necessary.

In 97, the aging emperor Nerva who favored older members of the Senate chose Pliny and Cornutus as prefects of the treasury of Saturn. They entered this office on 1 January 98. Pliny implies that, at least in his case, Trajan was involved in the choice, and this might be true (compare *Ep.* 10. 8. 3). However, although Trajan was almost co-emperor in 97, he was legate of Upper Germany and probably not much involved in such civilian appointments.

Pliny had held a post in the military treasury from 94 to 96, appointed by Domitian who recognized Pliny's financial ability. Ironically Pliny in the very letter in which he wrote of the appointment of Cornutus as curator of the Aemilian road disclaims interest in the business that occupied him on one of his estates and claims devotion to literature (*Ep.* 5. 14. 8). However, it is abundantly clear from his letters that he had real financial acumen whether in private or public business. Hence with such a colleague at the treasury of Saturn, Cornutus did not need to be a capable administrator and the appointment was routine rather than a special honor.

Pliny reached consular rank at the minimum age; Cornutus's consulship was long delayed. Cornutus held no priesthood to match Pliny's augurate. Pliny held a consular appointment in charge of the Tiber and the sewers at Rome—a post of the greatest importance because of the constant danger of floods in Rome. By contrast, Cornutus held a post often assigned to a *praetorius*, and although the *via Aemilia* was a trunk-line to the north, there is no evidence of extensive work on this road under Trajan.

The census in *Tres Galliae* was important, but Aquitania was the least important of the three Gauls, since Lugdunensis was far greater in area and Belgica was important as a supply area for the two consular imperial provinces that protected the Rhine frontier. Pliny was consular governor of Pontus and Bithynia with plenipotentiary power to reform the province that had deteriorated under proconsuls. The older Cornutus succeeded Pliny after the reforms had been implemented, and his title seems to indicate a province to which a *praetorius* was appointed. By virtue of longevity, Cornutus's name eventually appeared in the *sortitio* for one of the two consular proconsulships, and he governed Africa about 116–117.

Except for the governorship of Africa which Cornutus, in his middle seventies, could have refused on the grounds of age, his career under Trajan after his consulship was singularly undistinguished. He held three posts that normally would have been assigned to younger men of lower rank. The answer to this anomaly is to be found in the careers of the new emperor and his father. The elder Trajan was a *novus homo* from Baetica and was commander of a legion under Vespasian in the Jewish war. Soon consul he was raised to the patriciate by the imperial censors of 73, then assigned as legate of Syria whence he obtained the *ornamenta triumphalia*, the highest military honor possible for a senator, since full triumphs were restricted to members of the imperial family. Finally he was proconsul of Asia in 79–80.

The younger Trajan was a *vir militaris*—most unusually he spent ten years as a tribune of the soldiers,
including service in Syria with his father. As commander of a legion in Spain, he rushed his troops to
support Domitian when Saturninus revolted in Upper
Germany. He was honored with the eponymous consulship in 91. He must have been impressed with
Domitian's provincial policies, but for the sake of co-
operation with the Senate he accepted (or encouraged)
the denigration of the *imperator damnatus*. A story is
recorded (possibly apocryphal) of a comment to Trajan: "Domitian was a very evil man, but he had good
friends" (S. H. A. *Sev. Alex.* 65. 5).

It would seem clear that Trajan was more concerned
with military glory and less concerned with efficient
provincial government than Domitian, but he was a good
administrator and had extensive experience in the
provinces before he gained imperial power. Despite the
execration of Domitian's name, Trajan followed many
of Domitian's policies in the provinces. The correspondence between Pliny as governor of Pontus and Bithynia
(for example *Ep.* 10. 60) clarifies the extensive reten-
tion of Domitianic regulations. It might then be assumed
that in checking the imperial files Trajan found Domitian's estimate of Cornutus and agreed with it.

The bright prospects of Cornutus for a distinguished
career in the ranks of the Senate were dimmed after his
adlectio inter praetorios and his proconsulship in Gallia
Narbonensis. When he was for so long neglected under
Domitian, he could in public pose as indifferent to
power, but perhaps in private he may have wondered if
Domitian's judgment might be correct. Possibly he had
been snubbed by some senators because of his eastern
connections. In 98–100, he would have gained new
confidence, but subordination to a younger colleague
both as prefect and consul may have been unpleasant.
His later offices, held in his sixties, were not in accor-

dance with his rank as a senior consular senator until he held Africa at an age when most elderly senators had retired to their estates.

The inscription quoted above may give a clue to Cornutus's feelings after he returned from Africa and presumably retired to Tusculum. The altar was certainly raised at the site of his tomb, perhaps it stood in front of a structure containing his ashes in a funerary urn. Since the inscription was raised in accordance with his will, a manuscript copy of the text probably accompanied the will. The strange position, out of the normal order, of the Narbonese proconsulship could indicate to posterity the one earlier position in which he could feel a special pride. Thus we have a rather pathetic insight into an old man's pride in the bright spot in a rather undistinguished career.

XII.

VOCONIUS ROMANUS

amicus Plini

Pliny's great friend and coeval Gaius Licinius Marinus Voconius Romanus was a native of Saguntum (*CIL* 2. 3866). His father, C. Voconius Placidus, was a man of equestrian rank (*Ep*. 2. 13. 4) and had held distinguished posts in his municipality (*CIL* 2. 3865). He had married a woman from the local aristocracy (*Ep*. 2. 13. 4) and probably died before his son came of age. His widow married a C. Licinius Marinus, also of equestrian rank, who eventually adopted his stepson (*CIL* 2. 3866).

Since Voconius's family was of equestrian rank and quite well-to-do (*Ep*. 10. 4. 2), Voconius could look forward to the best education and the opportunities that his social standing could provide. He must have shown unusual promise as a student, for he was sent to Rome to complete his education, perhaps under the watchful eye of Quintilian. He quickly became friendly with Pliny who called him his close and intimate friend and added: "Who could be a more faithful friend or a more pleasant companion than Voconius?" (*Ep*. 2. 13. 6). No doubt, the Elder Pliny approved of their friendship, glad that his nephew would not be spending all his time in the company of elderly men such as Corellius Rufus, Avidius Quietus, and Verginius Rufus (*Ep*. 2. 1; 4. 17; 6. 29).

After completing his education, Voconius served an apprenticeship in the courts. Pliny thought that he had the ability to be a great pleader, for he noted: "His conversation is remarkable, and his charm is present even in his face and appearance. In addition to this, his mind is lofty, subtle, pleasant, and easily primed to plead cases" (*Ep.* 2. 13. 6–7). However, Voconius does not seem to have stayed in Rome or to have been eager to establish a career, for he returned to Saguntum (*Ep.* 2. 13. 4) and was absent for some years. When Pliny wrote to Javolenus Priscus, he was recommending Voconius, a man unknown to the recipient of the letter. There could be several reasons for returning to Spain: a desire to look after his property, homesickness, marriage. Perhaps too, Voconius disliked the bustle of Rome and the keen competition of political life on which Pliny thrived. Although he had the qualities to be a successful orator and politician, he may have preferred to be first in his own municipality than one of the many at Rome.

Voconius settled down to the life of the local squire. He married Popillia Rectina, a woman of good family, but she died quite young (*CIL* 2. 3866). Later Voconius became flamen of his province, Hither Spain, an office heavy in prestige and expense. His leisure hours may have been spent in literary composition. Like Pliny, he enjoyed writing letters. Pliny admired his epistles so much that he declared one would think that the Muses had written them in Latin (*Ep.* 2. 13. 7).

Nevertheless, Pliny looked upon his friend's way of life with some dissatisfaction. Apparently, he resolved that a man of Voconius's ability should have a political career and spared no effort to see that Voconius had one. Since Voconius's wife had died and he had no children nor any intention, so it seems, to remarry, his bachelor status was a disadvantage in seeking office. Accordingly, Pliny obtained the privileges granted to parents of three children for Voconius from Nerva (*Ep.* 2. 13. 8), so that he could stand for office earlier than the required age. Voconius made no use of this privilege, but Pliny seemed determined that Voconius should participate in political life. He wrote to Javolenus Priscus, requesting him to provide a position for Voconius on his staff, probably a military tribunate, if Voconius was still a knight (*Ep.* 2. 13). However, Priscus seems to have had no need of a man who had a fine voice and wrote lovely letters, for he refused Pliny's request. That might explain why Pliny, usually diplomatic, as revenge upon the man who denied his literate friend a post, sneered at Priscus at a recital of poetry (*Ep.* 6. 15).

Pliny was untiring on Voconius's behalf. He petitioned Nerva to raise Voconius to senatorial status, but the request was postponed because Voconius lacked the necessary amount of capital for the position (*Ep.* 10. 4. 2–3). After Nerva's death, Voconius's mother ceded her son enough property to meet the required sum and Pliny petitioned Trajan to raise Voconius's status (*Ep.* 10. 4. 1–2). It is more than likely that the emperor was willing to comply, for Pliny had made many more serious requests of Trajan that were granted (*Ep.* 10. 5–6, 10–13, 26, 94–95, 104–7). The answer for Voconius's inactivity lies in his character. If he was an Epicurean, he would not want an active political life and would prefer the quiet of his home and his literary pursuits. He must have finally made this clear to Pliny, who may have taken his reluctance for reticence and modesty. Pliny, once he understood his friend's mind, was forebearing enough not to interfere. Voconius's decision did not impair their friendship in the slightest, for when Pliny wrote to Voconius about his plans to prosecute Regulus, he concluded: "I have written about these things to you, for it was only right for you to know not only my words and deeds, but even my plans in view of our mutual friendship" (*Ep.* 1. 5. 17). Indeed, all his letters to Voconius show a deep affection and consideration for his friend. Voconius was not only a man to whom Pliny could confide his thoughts but also his emotions. When Verginius Rufus died, Pliny wrote a glorious obituary but then gave way to grief, unable to write of anything but Verginius (*Ep. 2. 1*). In Voconius, he found a sympathetic and patient ear.

If Voconius had no concern for a career of his own, he certainly displayed a lively interest in Pliny's. When Pliny delivered a speech of thanks to Trajan for his consulship, Voconius requested a copy, although Pliny remarked that he would have given him one without his asking (*Ep. 3. 13. 1*). Pliny felt that the subject of thanking the emperor for the consulship had many pitfalls, especially since the theme was a common one. He hoped that the reader would devote his attention to the stylistic devices and rhetorical turns in the speech. Voconius was asked to make any alterations that he saw fit, for Pliny trusted his judgment (*Ep. 3. 13. 2–5*). It is doubtful that Pliny would send Voconius the speech unless he was planning to enlarge and publish it. Voconius would know this without being told, especially as he was asked to make corrections. He was pleased that Pliny thought him a suitable critic of oratory and Pliny was pleased that Voconius was so interested in his work.

When Pliny sent Voconius his speech, *pro Attia Viriola*, he enthusiastically described the circumstances of the case, the tension in the courtroom, and his very grand Ciceronian delivery (*Ep. 6. 33*). It is clear that Pliny was making every effort to give Voconius the background material, so that he would enjoy reading the speech which was sent without the asking. There is an interesting sidelight to the letter, for Pliny remarked: "In conclusion, certain of my friends are wont to consider this speech (and I tell you the truth) the *de corona* of my orations. Whether this is actually true, you will be able to judge, as you have committed them all to memory so you will be able to compare them with this one when you read it alone" (*Ep. 6. 33. 11*). Voconius had been collecting Pliny's speeches and had requested his friend to send him copies. Voconius's admiration of Pliny's speeches equalled Calpurnia's admiration of his verses (*Ep.* 4. 19).

Not long afterwards, Voconius decided to leave Spain and to visit Italy, for Pliny wrote a letter, describing the source of the Clitumnus River as he was sure Voconius had not seen it and really ought to (*Ep.* 8. 8). This letter is more of a literary exercise than a personal note. Perhaps Pliny was imitating one of Voconius's compositions or wished to provide him with an excuse to stay in Italy a little longer. If so, he was unsuccessful, for his next letter was addressed to Voconius, now back at home, building a villa by the sea (*Ep.* 9. 7. 1). Pliny joked that they had a point in common since he was building by the shores of Lake Como. He digressed on his two favorite villas there, which he called Tragedy and Comedy, names that must have amused Voconius (*Ep.* 9. 7. 2–5).

The last letter to Voconius shows that their friendship was as strong and devoted as ever. Three of Voconius's letters had reached Pliny after a long delay and he was relieved to receive them. He marvelled at his friend's literate style, for he called his epistles all very well expressed and affectionate (*Ep.* 9. 28. 1). The first letter contained an enclosure to be forwarded to the Empress Plotina. There was also a request to aid Popilius Artemisius, probably a freedman of his late wife. Pliny promised to carry out both requests. Voconius also complained of a poor grape harvest, but Pliny consoled him, saying that the same misfortune had fallen upon him as well (*Ep.* 9. 28. 2). The second letter caused Pliny no end of joy. Voconius was writing a biography of Pliny. He playfully begged to be allowed to read it, insisting that since Voconius had read his speeches, he ought to be able to read Voconius's works. He was surely not afraid of what Voconius might say but anxious to read about himself. Voconius had also written that once he heard of Pliny's arrangements, possibly a reference to his appointment as governor of Pontus and Bithynia, he would join him (*Ep.* 9. 28. 3–4). It is possible that he did go to Bithynia with Pliny, for the letter implies that he was seriously thinking of leaving Spain. The Greek East would be greatly tempting to the literary-minded Voconius.

In the third letter, Voconius expressed some surprise that Pliny's speech on Clarius's behalf was fuller than when Voconius had heard him deliver it (*Ep.* 9. 28. 5). This speech would date to Voconius's stay in Italy (*Ep.* 8. 8). What better way for Voconius to honor Pliny than by listening to him plead? Apparently, Pliny's custom of extensive revision surprised Voconius, for having few opportunities to hear Pliny speak, he could hardly be expected to know whether it was the actual speech delivered verbatim or a much revised edition that was sent to him, unless Pliny informed him of the fact.

If Voconius went with Pliny to Bithynia, he must have gone as companion and friend, for he does not seem to have been a man of administrative talents. If he was in Bithynia, he may have been present when Pliny died. Afterwards, he probably returned to Saguntum and spent the remainder of his life there. Pliny's death created a gap in his life, for a true friend is hard to find. In a sense, their friendship could be compared to that of Cicero and Atticus. But Voconius was a much better and finer Atticus, for his friendship with Pliny was based on mutual admiration and unbroken devotion. Unlike Cicero's Atticus, Voconius needed no Nepos to write an *apologia pro sua uita*.

The career of Voconius illustrates a common phenomenon—the provincial aristocrat. Since Rome was timocratic, men of property and local eminence in the province were favored by the central administration. Many of these men were ambitious, cultivated their connections in Rome, and rose to prominence as equestrian officials or gained admission to the Senate. Voconius represents those who preferred a life of distinction in their own homeland and lived in more leisurely fashion as landed gentry.

XIII.
JULIUS GENITOR
rhetor

The education of scions of the aristocracy in antiquity was a serious matter. Therefore, when Pliny's good friend Junius Mauricus wrote to Pliny that his nephews needed the services of a rhetor and requested his friend to find him a suitable one, Pliny replied that he would like nothing better than to find a tutor for the children of Arulenus Rusticus, and that he had already set himself conscientiously to the task before he wrote his reply. Pliny took his task quite seriously and wished to find the best teacher possible, for he must have realized that the knowledge of good speaking was essential for political and oratorical fame. In order to find the right teacher, he visited all the schools where oratory was taught and listened to each of the lecturers. It was an extremely time-consuming task, for Pliny wrote to Mauricus that he had not yet heard all of the speakers but would write when he had (*Ep.* 2. 18. 1–4).

Whom did Pliny recommend? The answer may be provided in Pliny's response to a letter from Corellia Hispulla. She too had asked Pliny to find a suitable teacher for her son. His earlier education, as befitted the grandson of Corellius Rufus, had been with private tutors. The boy was to attend school for the first time and his mother was afraid that he might go astray. Pliny gently soothed her fears, declaring that they would find a rhetor whose school combined strict training, good manners, and high moral standards. Julius Genitor was such a rhetor. Pliny assured Corellia that his respect for Genitor did not blind his judgment (*Ep.* 3. 3. 1–5). He warmly praised Genitor's character and ability:

> He is of serious disposition and morally faultless, perhaps even a little too blunt and gruff, when comparison is made to the license of our own times. You will be able to trust the testimony of witnesses as to the power of his eloquence. For his ability to speak is obviously recognized when put on display. (Ep. 3. 3. 5–6)

Genitor's origins are obscure. It may be speculated that he was the son of moderately well-to-do Italians. As a boy, he must have shown unusual aptitude for literature and declamation, so that his parents encouraged his talents with the thought that if he became a teacher, he would earn a decent living by their standards. As a rhetor, he enjoyed some success, for he had acquired a reputation good enough to draw Pliny's attention.

If Genitor was gruff and tart, he had good reason. Juvenal in his seventh satire luridly describes the troubles of those who taught rhetoric, the students who complain that they have learned nothing, the parents who refuse to pay the teacher's salary, the rascally slaves who pilfer a bit of the rhetorician's wages for themselves, and worst of all, the students who enjoy beating their teachers who were presumably of lower social rank and therefore unable to defend themselves. Some, like Quintilian, might enjoy better fortune in their profession, but Juvenal glumly noted that fortune ruled the outcome (7. 150–214). It can be assumed that Genitor may have suffered some of these indignities and resented them bitterly.

Pliny's opinion of Genitor's abilities is surely accurate, for he was a fine speaker in his own right. Furthermore, there is no reason to believe that Pliny abused the trust Corellia had placed in him when he declared that he would answer for Genitor and that Corellia's son would learn nothing but what would benefit him (*Ep.* 3. 3. 6).

It would be interesting to know who recommended Genitor to Pliny. Artemidorus, the philosopher, is an attractive choice. Pliny considered him a man of complete integrity (*Ep.* 3. 11. 5–6) and would certainly consider any advice he might offer. And Artemidorus was a good friend of Genitor, for when Pliny wrote to Genitor about his generosity to the philosopher during the Domitianic terror, he called Artemidorus "our friend" (*Ep.* 3. 11. 1). Artemidorus may well have wished to impress upon Genitor what type of man Pliny was and praised him in such effusive terms that he both delighted and embarrassed Pliny into writing an account of his actions (*Ep.* 3. 11. 1, 5, 8–9).

Genitor did not disappoint his sponsor's expectations, for the two men remained friends. When a promising young pupil died, Pliny wrote a short note of consolation. The gruff Genitor is revealed to have been a more kindly teacher than Pliny had implied and extremely devoted to his serious students (*Ep.* 7. 30. 1). Genitor must have been heartbroken at the boy's death, for a student who had both the ability and enthusiasm for oratory must have been as rare as a white crow.

Pliny discussed his oratorical productions with Genitor, for in the same letter he delared that he was discouraged with his *On Avenging Helvidius*, even though Genitor had compared it to Demosthenes' *Against Meidias*. But the strain of city business and the running of his estates was probably the cause of Pliny's low literary morale (*Ep.* 7. 30. 2–5). Obviously, he thought highly enough of Genitor to console him and unburden his own troubles at the same time. No doubt, Genitor appreciated Pliny's concern and wrote a reply, urging patience and declaring that Pliny's speech was really much better than its author thought.

The last exchange is somewhat strained. Genitor had attended a grand dinner party at which mimes, clowns, and dancers had performed, much to his disgust. Pliny agreed that such amusements were not much to his liking either, but many people thought his delight in readers, musicians, and actors incomprehensible. Therefore, he urged tolerance of other people's pleasures in order to win indulgence for one's own (*Ep.* 9. 17).

Pliny's tone is somewhat sharp. He may have been annoyed at Genitor's playing Cato. Perhaps too, he felt that Genitor was out of place criticizing the hospitality of a man of higher rank, especially if that man was a friend of Pliny. But he was not so angry that he could not write a short sermon on the toleration of tastes. Genitor probably took the hint and in the future refrained from condemning the amusements of others, especially those of Pliny's friends.

Not much is known of Genitor's later life. However, it may be guessed that he continued to teach rhetoric for many years and enjoyed an excellent reputation. The importance of *rhetores* in the imperial educational system was paramount. They taught the art of persuasive speech, and such training was essential for the sons of equestrian and senatorial families, if they were to maintain or improve their positions. The uses of oratory were most obvious in the courts, but in the Senate, in imperial councils, and in many other situations the cogent speaker had a special advantage. Quintilian who gained membership in the Senate under Domitian was the most notable of these *rhetores*, but there were many such as Genitor who, although competent teachers, were socially inferior to the families of their pupils.

XIV.

EUPHRATES

sophistes philosophicus

Euphrates of Tyre merited a character sketch in one of Pliny's letters, and there are two casual references to him by Epictetus and Fronto, but his quarrel with Apollonius of Tyana gives him a greater claim to fame. Philostratus's biography of Apollonius provides a fairly substantial amount of information about his Neo-pythagorean archenemy.

Euphrates was probably born about 45, for when Pliny in the early eighties served as a military tribune in Syria, he visited Euphrates and made every effort to win his friendship (*Ep.* 1. 10. 1–3). His behavior sounds like that of an eager young man paying court to a mature man, fifteen to twenty years his senior. It may be guessed that Euphrates belonged to the local aristocracy. As a young man, he had shown a keen interest in oratory and philosophy that his parents were willing to encourage as long as he did not neglect the family property. He appears to have adhered to the Stoic philosophy, for Fronto wrote that Musonius Rufus was his teacher (Haines 2. 50). Undoubtedly, Euphrates traveled throughout the Greek East to study with the best teachers and to sharpen his own skills. In the end, he returned to his native city and settled down to the life of the gentleman Sophist-philosopher. He was a man of considerable means as well as reputation, for otherwise he would have been unable to marry the daughter of Pompeius Julianus, the leading citizen of his province.

Although Pliny insisted that he had won the girl's hand because of his high character (*Ep.* 1. 10. 8), wealthy men do not give their daughters to philosophers without means.

Euphrates is one of the arch-villains of Philostratus's imaginative *Vita Apollonii*. The two men appear to have become implacable enemies at Alexandria when Euphrates advised Vespasian to restore the Republic, while Apollonius urged him to become emperor. Philostratus records the long-winded debate that is probably a pastiche, complete with all the arguments used by schoolboys in their declamations (*VA* 5. 27–39). The rest of the biography finds Euphrates intriguing against the saintly Apollonius, undermining his reputation through slander, and eventually getting him arraigned before Domitian on the charge of being a magician (*VA* 7. 36). These stories are extremely suspect. Vespasian at Alexandria had far more important things to do than listen to philosophers theorize. His allies were invading Italy and he was eager to join them. He had long made up his mind to be emperor and did not need the advice of men who were inexperienced in government or military affairs. As for the charge of magic, Apollonius may have instigated it, although even the charge is dubious. However, if the case was tried, it was certainly not judged by Domitian, who would not bother with so trivial a case, but before a praetor who would have dismissed the case with the contempt that it deserved.

Apollonius's letters give the real issue between the two men. The Pythagorean thoroughly disapproved of Euphrates's way of life, for he wrote bitingly that Euphrates was too wealthy, he charged a fee for instruction, he acted like a mercenary businessman, he fawned upon the rich, and perhaps most important of all he looked down upon Apollonius's ascetic way of life as well as his Pythagorean beliefs (Ap. *Ep.* 1–8, 14–18, 50–52, 60). The charges were probably exaggerated, for it would be very unlikely that two such intelligent and discerning people as Pliny and Epictetus would fail to recognize Euphrates's true character if he were the materialistic monster that Apollonius declared he was. It can be said with reasonable certainty that the quarrel between the two stemmed from diametrically opposed temperaments. Apollonius was a mystic, an ascetic (*VA* 1. 8, 10–11), and had he lived when Christianity held sway, he almost surely would have been canonized as a saint. Consequently, he despised Euphrates, who favored living comfortably. Furthermore, Euphrates's being a Stoic would not please a philosopher of a rival school. Indeed, the letters may have been forged by Philostratus to confirm some of the more fantastic portions of his biography.

Epictetus, the great Stoic philosopher of the early empire, had mixed feelings about Euphrates. He relates, somewhat tongue-in-cheek, a conversation that he had with him. Euphrates stated rather smugly that he did not flaunt the fact that he was a philosopher but tried to act the philosopher for himself alone, thus drawing no attention to himself, or if he behaved badly he did the case of philosophy no harm. He further told Epictetus that people wondered how it was that he lived on familiar terms with all the philosophers but did not play the role of a philosopher. His answer was that he wished to be recognized as a philosopher by his actions, not by his outward appearance (*Disc.* 4. 8. 17–20). Although Epictetus may not have considered Euphrates a true philosopher, he had no reservations about him as a speaker, for he noted, perhaps with a sigh, "Who indeed can speak as he does?" (*Disc.* 3. 15. 8).

Pliny thought highly of Euphrates. He had met him while serving as a military tribune in Syria. He liked him immediately and made every effort to win his affection. Euphrates took a liking to the young tribune and saw in him great promise, although Pliny modestly asserted that he had not fulfilled Euphrates's expectations (*Ep.* 1. 10. 1–3).

If Euphrates came to Rome soon thereafter, he would have been forced to leave with all the other philosophers, including Artemidorus whom Pliny had also met in Syria (*Ep.* 3. 11), when Domitian exiled them in 93. Apparently, he returned during Nerva's reign.

Pliny enthusiastically described his eloquence, for he wrote: "He argues subtly, in a dignified manner, his language properly embellished. Frequently he attains the sublimity and breadth of Plato. His speech is both eloquent and diversified, and his very charm actually attracts and captivates even those who do not share his view" (*Ep.* 1. 10. 5). Nor was Pliny the only one impressed by Euphrates's eloquence. Epictetus had praised him highly and Fronto remembered him as a man who had won glory, not only through his wisdom, but through great eloquence (Haines 2. 50–52).

Pliny also admired Euphrates's imposing appearance. The Sophist was tall and distinguished looking, with long hair and a great white beard. However, Pliny felt that he had no need of these natural advantages, since Euphrates was so eloquent. He sincerely admired his modest manner, his blameless life, and his humanity, and the fact that Euphrates had lavished much care on the education of his children deeply impressed Pliny (*Ep.* 1. 10. 6–8).

Pliny, burdened with offices, often sought solace in Euphrates's company. The philosopher comforted him, declaring that he was putting the philosophical life into practice. However, Pliny felt that attending official business was not nearly so good as listening to Euphrates and learning from him. He even advised a friend to let Euphrates take him in hand and polish him, presumably in oratory (*Ep.* 1. 10. 9–11). Apparently, even a fine orator like Pliny felt that he could learn, although he was an experienced speaker.

Euphrates

Euphrates lived for some years after Pliny's letter was written. He continued to teach, his most famous pupil being the haughty Timocrates of Heraclia (Philostr. *VS* 1. 25. 536). However, as the years advanced and he grew older his health was increasingly afflicted by disease. He wished to die and in 119 Hadrian permitted him to drink hemlock in consideration of his old age and illness (Dio 69. 8. 3). Although he had no enthusiastic biographer such as Philostratus, the very solid testimony of men like Pliny, Epictetus, and Fronto does him far more justice than the romance of Philostratus does for Apollonius of Tyana.

Speculative philosophers appeared early in Greece, and at the height of Greek culture Plato and Aristotle dominated the intellectual field. The philosophical systems of the Hellenistic world, particularly the Stoic and Epicurean, were largely derivative. Latin writers who adapted Greek philosophy for the more practical uses of the Romans did not display originality : such were Cicero (a skeptic with Stoic leanings), Lucretius (an Epicurean), and the younger Seneca (a Stoic). The Greek teachers of philosophy in the period under discussion were not original, but flavored Sophistic eloquence with philosophy. Their influence on their Roman pupils and patrons was not strong. The most notable was Dio Chrysostomus whose discourses are preserved, but it is doubtful that the Emperor Trajan with whom he claimed intimacy was steered from his anti-intellectual stance by Dio's comments on kingship. Euphrates's friends were less distinguished and he was more typical. It was not long before Christianity became dominant in East and West. Original thinkers, such as Origen and St. Augustine turned to theology, and soon the schools of philosophy were closed.

XV.

POMPEIUS FALCO

vir militaris

Of the fourteen emperors from 27 B.C. to A.D. 138, only five were competent generals in the field: Tiberius, the three Flavians, and Trajan. The proportion of senators in this period with genuine military ability as commanders (*viri militares*) was even smaller. The most notable was Domitius Corbulo, father of the Empress Domitia, whose exploits under Nero are recorded by Tacitus (*Ann.* 15. 1–17). Much later Ammianus Marcellinus cited Corbulo as an example of the great military heroes of the past (29. 5. 4). Under Trajan, another of these *viri militares* was Q. Pompeius Falco.

Pliny, who addressed four letters to Falco, mentioned him in another, and Marcus Aurelius told of a visit to his estate. From these six items in the literary sources there is little to indicate the importance of Falco's career that can be reconstructed from a surprising number of inscriptions.

When Falco was *tribunus plebis* in 97, or when he was *designatus* in the preceding year, he inquired of Pliny whether he should appear as attorney in the courts while holding the office that entitled its holder to the right of intercession, which is to halt court proceedings by saying *veto* ("I forbid"). Pliny replied (1. 23) by saying that he had refrained from pleading cases when he was tribune, but Falco should decide for himself (as *sapiens uir*) whether the office was an empty shadow or a sacrosanct power. To be sure imperial *tribunicia potestas* had reduced the *tribuni plebis* to an exercise in futility. This is the only indication that Falco was *patronus* and, therefore, presumably had been trained under a rhetor, possibly the notable Quintilian, who had been Pliny's *magister* (2. 14. 9–12; 6. 6. 3). The reference to him as *sapiens uir* seems to imply a wider scope to Falco's education. Also implied is his earlier election as quaestor and with this election senatorial status.

In a letter written a decade later (9. 13), Pliny narrates his rather harsh attack in the Senate on Publicius Certus, who had been responsible for the execution of the younger Helvidius Priscus, with whose family and Stoic friends Pliny was on good terms. Fabricius Veiento, *ter consul* and Domitian's trusted adviser, attempted to defend Certus, but was shouted down. Falco as tribune tried unsuccessfully to give Veiento a hearing (9. 13. 19). Pliny refers to him as Murena, and the inscriptions prove that this was part of his name, although it does not otherwise occur in the literary references. Two hints occur here of Falco's favor with two emperors, Domitian and Nerva. He interceded for a favorite of the earlier emperor and was in accord with the action of Nerva who did not allow Pliny to proceed with his attack upon Certus.

About 104, Pliny began to relieve his cares as attorney in the courts and as civilian official by writing light verse. He regales Falco with an account of a *recitatio* of similar poems by Sentius Augurinus (4. 27). Such innocent amusement had occupied the leisure moments of educated aristocrats from the days of Q. Lutatius Catulus (consul, 102 B.C.) to the time of the imperial dilettante Hadrian. Fortunately most of this poetic effusion is lost. The tone of the letter indicates that Falco was interested in amateur poetry and might even have been a practitioner. He is obviously out of Italy, but Pliny gives us no hint of his position.

Soon, in 106 or 107, Pliny recommended a young friend for appointment as *tribunus militum* by Falco (7. 22). This is the only indication by Pliny that Falco held a military command. The final letter, probably in 108 when Falco was consul, was written from the country to Rome. In it Pliny speaks of revising some orations and of his activities on a country estate (9. 15). Both items fit a letter from one landholder and attorney to another.

Many years later, Falco appears in a letter written by young M. Aurelius to his mentor Fronto (*ad M. Caes.* 2. 11; Haines 1. 140–41):

> I remember that three years ago my father and I were returning from the vintage season and we turned aside to the estate of Pompeius Falco. There I saw a tree with many branches which Falco called by its special Greek name *catachanna*.

Falco had outlived Domitian, Nerva, Trajan, and Hadrian, for the letter is dated 143. At about the age of 70, he was on such good terms with Antoninus Pius that the emperor with his precocious heir could stop for a friendly visit. His was a fruitful old age since the tree (*catachanna*) was apparently some type of fruit tree. Falco's normal cognomen is unusual, possibly he did not establish his interest in farming late in life and the name could have been given to him for such interests, since *falx* ("sickle, pruning hook, scythe") was a very common Roman farming implement. Here we may recall Cicero's quotation from Caecilius Statius (*Sen.* 24) about the old man who "plants trees to profit another generation."

Numerous extant inscriptions outline an extensive career for Falco and these with some inscriptions of his wife and their descendants mark his family as important in the history of the second century. He was probably a member of a family of Hierapolis Castabala in Cilicia where a bilingual inscription gives his earlier career

(*ILS* 1036). He was almost certainly *novus homo*, since various inscriptions of his granddaughter Falconilla list her consular forbears, but do not list Falco's father (for example *ILS* 1105). His family, whatever its origin, was surely wealthy and he probably was educated in Rome. He was born about 70, since his praetorship was in 99 or 100 under Trajan.

The Cilician inscription and one from his estate at Tarracina on the coast of Latium (*ILS* 1035) give a list of all of his official positions, and complete his name. In the second century, multiplication of names marks the interconnections of aristocratic families. His full nomenclature is Q. Roscius Coelius Murena Silius Decianus Vibullius Pius Iulius Eurycles Herclanus Pompeius Falco. He cannot match his polyonymous grandson (consul, 169) who had thirty-eight names. Most interesting are the fifth and sixth that indicate a connection with Silius Decianus (consul in 94), the elder son of the poet Silius Italicus. Though Falco was the first in his family to hold the consulship and may have been the first of senatorial rank, his father apparently already had important ties in the senatorial ranks.

Falco's first three positions were held under Domitian and probably indicate the sponsorship of the emperor. He was a member of the board of ten with minor judicial functions, which was appropriate for a young man who was an attorney in the courts. He then was *tribunus militum* of *legio X Fretensis* that was stationed in Judea, an imperial province since 70. As quaestor, probably in 95, he entered the Senate. He may have been *candidatus Caesaris* (that is, of Domitian), although the inscriptions do not specify. His office as tribune of the people was followed by the praetorship—the terminology *inter ciues et peregrinos* is an amplification of the republican title *praetor peregrinus*, whose holder presided over the court involving civil suits between a citizen and a foreigner or between two foreigners.

Trajan recognized Falco's military potential and as *praetorius* he was given the command of *legio V Macedonica*, which was to participate in the First Dacian War. Trajan left Rome in March of 101 to command the Dacian operations. One of Trajan's consular legates was Sosius Senecio (consul in 99, 107), and Falco surely gained favor then with his future father-in-law. With victory attained by 102, Falco was back in Rome, decorated by Trajan for his service in Dacia. Two appointments to *provinciae praetoriae*, that is imperial provinces garrisoned with one legion, followed. The first was Lycia-Pamphylia that borders on Cilicia, the second Judea where he was governor and commander of *legio X Fretensis* in which he had earlier served as tribune. This latter post was especially important since there were probably already signs of the Jewish unrest that broke out in revolt late in Trajan's reign. These two posts kept Falco in the East for about five or six years.

Falco's marriage to Sosia Polla probably took place on his return from Judea. Good service was rewarded by the suffect consulship in 108, and then or soon thereafter by membership in the *quindecimviri sacris faciundis*, one of the four great colleges of priests. There followed appointment as *curator viae Traianae*. The streets of Rome and minor roads in Italy were under the care of junior officials or *equites*, but the major roads were supervised by *praetorii* or *consulares* as *curatores*. This appointment does not seem important enough for a man of Falco's accomplishments.

Speculation may explain Trajan's action. From inscriptions on the *miliaria*, it is clear that Trajan intended to complete major work on the *via Appia* from Rome to Brundisium, probably in anticipation of the military necessities of present and future eastern campaigns. Road construction in the provinces, especially the imperial provinces, was closely allied to military operations, and many roads were built by troops in time of peace.

No *curator viae Appiae* is known for this period, and it makes sense to assume that Falco had charge of the whole route. The most exacting tasks were the nineteen mile swampy stretch beyond Tarracina (*decennovium*), and the re-routing and widening of a further portion nearer Brundisium. At all events by 112–114, coin issues commemorate the completion of the work and use the name *via Traiana* (*BMC* 3. 208–15). Thus Trajan had assigned a task that called for the engineering skill of a *vir militaris*. Let us hope that Falco and Sosia found time to relax in their suburban villa at Tarracina. It was probably in these years that their son, Q. Pompeius Sosius Priscus (consul in 149), was born.

Soon special imperial assignments sent Falco far from Italy with arduous duties, and Sosia probably remained in Italy to care for their son and the family property. Both appointments were to provinces where military competence was essential. He was consular legate of Trajan in Lower Moesia during the period when Trajan was carrying on his ill-conceived Parthian War. He was consular legate of Hadrian in Britain at a time of turmoil. *Legati consulares* were assigned to imperial provinces garrisoned by more than one legion and were the commanders with *legati legionum* acting under their orders. Such appointments in troubled areas by two emperors who were experts in military affairs were indications of Falco's reputation.

Falco's career is especially rich in epigraphical evidence at this time. The inscription to Falco at Hierapolis Castabala in Cilicia dates in the first part of the period, since the appointment to Britain is not included. In it Falco's career is given in Latin. The Greek in the last five lines indicates the circumstances of the dedication:

> Aulus Laberius Camerinus and Laberius Camerinus, his son, centurion of the fifth Macedonian legion, set this up with their own money, to honor their friend and benefactor Pompeius Falco.

Thus the connection seems to go back to the time when the younger man served under Falco who was *legatus* of *legio V Macedonica* in the First Dacian War. Their friendship and Falco's patronage probably continued when Falco was governor of Lycia-Pamphylia. Obviously the Camerini, holding *civitas Romana*, were important men in this Cilician city.

Falco's term in Lower Moesia is dated by two inscriptions raised by him in honor of Trajan. These include in the emperor's titulature at Adamclisi his twentieth tribunician power in 115–116 (*CIL* 3. 12470) and at Tomi his twenty-first in 116–117 (*CIL* 3. 7537). Thus only 116 is firmly attested, but he was probably governor for several years. The later inscription is especially interesting since it comes from the architrave of a small building in Tomi.

A sepulchral inscription of a freedman of Falco was found at Oescus where *legio V Macedonica* was stationed in the First Dacian War (*CIL* 3. 7433). It is uncertain to which period in Falco's life this should be dated. Two undated military inscriptions are from Calachioi in Dacia (*AE* 1934, 112) and Durastorum in Moesia (*AE* 1936, 14). Two fragmentary architraval inscriptions from Tomi include reference to Falco (*AE* 1962, 145) and give additional evidence of his building activities as governor. An acephalous *titulus honorarius* was raised at Tomi some years after Falco left, since his appointment to Britain is mentioned. The inscription is cut on a limestone altar that was set up by "Annaeus Vibianus in accordance with the will of his brother Annaeus Vibianus" (*AE* 1957, 336, lines 8–10). These two brothers, clients of Falco, were surely soldiers or civilian officials under Falco in Moesia. If soldiers, on discharge they remained in Tomi.

Since Falco was in Moesia while Trajan was campaigning beyond the Euphrates, it was natural that his headquarters should be in Tomi on the Black Sea where he could help forestall any attempt by the Parthians to bypass the main forces and attack from the rear. At the same time, Hadrian was consular legate of Syria, and although he had not been designated as Trajan's heir to imperial power, many Roman senators must have looked on him as the logical successor. Consequently I suspect that duplicates of Falco's reports on the Danubian frontier went to Antioch. Falco would be aware that Rome was not yet ready for an emperor from the East, and so he would not be suspect in Hadrian's eyes. Moreover Falco seems to have added smooth diplomacy to his administrative and military skill.

The inscription from Tarracina proves that the Moesian command terminated before Trajan's death in 117 and that the appointment to Britain was made by Hadrian. This appointment made good sense since Roman forces in Britain had suffered serious reverses. The new emperor chose an able commander whom he could trust. In the "conspiracy of the four consulars," three of the men killed were Trajanic generals and consequently consular *viri militares* were in short supply. Falco probably assumed this office in 118.

The victory of the Hadrianic legions in Britain in 119 celebrated in the famous Jarrow inscription (*RIB* 1051) was probably not complete, and Falco was not replaced until 122. In the spring of that year after a tour of the area of the Rhine, Hadrian crossed to Britain. I suspect he waited until he could be assured that his legate had made Britain safe for an emperor. Hadrian for all his knowledge of military administration and his tours of the empire inspecting military establishments was not a *vir militaris*, but a poet, scholar, architect, and intellectual.

The evidence for the termination of Falco's British command is found in an unusual *diploma militare* of 17 July 122 in which troops were discharged from units *quae sunt in Brittania sub A. Platorio Nepote*. However, they are also described as receiving honorable discharge (*honesta missione*) through Pompeius Falco (*CIL* 16. 69). Nepos (consul in 119) was a friend of the emperor and had just completed a term as consular legate of Lower Germany (*ILS* 1052) where Hadrian had been touring. I suspect that he accompanied the emperor in the crossing and took over from Falco in the first half of 122. Lower Germany at this time was not a trouble spot, and the discharge of veterans in Britain may well indicate cessation of hostilities there. According to the biographer of Hadrian, Nepos reorganized administration and built a wall (S. H. A. *Hadr.* 11. 2) that, however, took its name from the emperor and is still mentioned at times by British archaeologists.

The delay in being relieved in Britain while Hadrian was presumably climbing a German mountain or writing a poem on Rhine wine brought Falco back to Rome too late for his name to be entered in the *sortitio* for Asia or Africa for the consular proconsulship of 122–123, for which he was due by age and distinction. These two provinces gave the governor less power than that of a consular legate in an imperial province, but tradition was so strong in the Roman senatorial class that these two provinces were more prestigious. In the *sortitio* for 123–124, Falco drew Asia. Perhaps his presumed eastern origin was the reason, especially since *viri militares* seem to have been more frequently granted Africa at this time. To be sure *sortitio* was supposed to represent the will of the gods, but rigging the *sortes* would not worry the Senate.

The extra year between provincial offices allowed Falco to become reacquainted with his wife and son who accompanied him to Asia. The boy probably enjoyed the sights, and by the middle of the second century he and his daughter Falconilla seem to have indulged in a grand tour since inscriptions were raised to her in

Numidian Cirta (*ILS* 1105), in Athens (*AE* 1947, 80), and in Minturnae (*AE* 1935, 26). Since three are preserved, it is likely that there were more. I have guessed that Falco took his son with him, but the presence of his wife is proved by an inscription, probably on the base of a statue he set up for her: "To Sosia Polla, Pompeius Falco, proconsul of Asia, (set this up) to his most sacred wife" (*ILS* 1037). Sosia was also honored by Phrygian Apamea with two statues—the inscriptions are preserved (*ILS* 8820; *IGRR* 4. 779). In both she is noted not only as wife of the proconsul but also as the daughter of Sosius Senecio whose ancestors came from Asia, probably from Apamea, which was in the province of Asia.

Falco was honored at Ephesus where a white marble base that probably held a statue was found with an honorary inscription to the proconsul (*AE* 1972, 577). Two delegates of the council and the people of *colonia Flavia Neapolis Samaria* set this up to the proconsul Falco "saviour and benefactor." Such magniloquence is common in eastern inscriptions.

The remainder of Falco's life was more leisurely. He held no further provincial appointments, but he probably fulfilled his priestly duties and attended the Senate even after the age of sixty or sixty-five, when he would no longer be under an obligation to do so. Perhaps he, as a senior consular senator, exercised real influence not only on his fellow senators but also on Hadrian, Pius, and Marcus. It is not known how long he survived after 143. If the tree mentioned by young Marcus was as its name seems to indicate a product of extensive grafting, Falco may have extended an already long life by the solace of light agricultural tasks.

It was during this period of semiretirement that the long inscription with full details of his later offices was erected at Tarracina (earlier name Anxur). Since the

offices are given in descending order, the break at the end
has been filled in for early offices from the Cilician
inscription. The estate probably came to Falco by inheritance since here the poet Martial visited his patron
Frontinus (10. 58), grandfather of Falco's wife Sosia.
Three other inscriptions are possibly from this time: a
fragmentary honorary inscription in Rome (*CIL* 6.
31752); the grant of a burial plot to a friend or client
in Rome (*AE* 1921, 90); and a similar grant at Tusculum (*AE* 14. 2692) where he probably had an estate.

It is not amiss to quote here the first five lines of the
Cirtan inscription, mentioned above, to his son's daughter (*ILS* 1105):

> To Sosia Falconilla, daughter of Pompeius Sosius
> Priscus consul, granddaughter of Quintus Pompeius
> Falco consul, great-granddaughter of Quintus Sosius
> Senecio twice consul, great-great-granddaughter of
> Sextus Julius Frontinus thrice consul . . .

Latin did not use our clumsy phrases: instead *neptis,
proneptis, abneptis.*

A career such as Falco's tempts speculation. Hadrian
severely disapproved of the Parthian War and his first
action as emperor was to abandon the new provinces
beyond the Euphrates and concentrate on trouble in the
Danubian area. The fourth century epitomator Eu-
tropius after mentioning Hadrian's action in the East
added: "His friends deterred him when he attempted
to do the same thing with Dacia" (8. 6). Falco could
have been one of those *amici.*

Falco even in his earlier years must have united
diplomacy and charm. Although favored briefly by Domitian he was in the good graces of Trajan and Pliny.
He was able to make a smooth transition from two men
so different as Trajan and Hadrian. He was on familiar
terms with Antoninus. He gained Sosius Senecio as
father-in-law. The union of a legal career and a military

career indicates adaptability to circumstances. In sum a remarkable man—he might have been a better emperor than Hadrian, and he certainly illustrates the type of man upon whom the peace and security of the empire depended under good and bad emperors.

XVI.
PLOTINA
imperatrix philosopha

Pompeia Plotina is an elusive figure. Almost nothing is known about her life before she became empress. Where she was born and when are not known, although guesses can be made. She may have been born as early as 53/54, and if this date is correct, Plotina's marriage to a man of her own years was unusual indeed. However, Pliny's *Panegyricus* describes a sedate and mature lady, one who had been married for a considerable length of time (83). Her place of origin has provoked considerable discussion. Hadrian dedicated a basilica to her after her death at Nemausus (S. H. A. *Hadr.* 12. 2), so Gallia Narbonensis has been suggested. However, Hadrian may have received news of her death there and this could explain why the basilica was built in that city. Spain has been considered as her birthplace because she married into Trajan's family that was of Spanish extraction. Crete has also been suggested on the basis of inscriptions (*IC* 1. 27–31). It is possible too that her family belonged to the aristocracy of southern Italy, for two wax tablets discovered at Herculaneum and dated 69/70 are inscribed with the name of *Ulpia Plotina* (*AE* 1955, 198). It might be guessed that Ulpia Plotina was the daughter of the elder Trajan by a previous marriage, and that Plotina was a niece of that wife, but nothing certain is known of her parents.

When Plotina came of marriageable age, the elder Trajan probably selected her for his son. A substantial dowry may have been a prime attraction, but the elder Trajan may have been impressed by her good character and realized that she would be a worthy helpmate for his son. Furthermore, he must have realized that after his son had fulfilled his military apprenticeship, an early marriage would facilitate access to the higher offices of the *cursus honorum*. Plotina may have been attracted to her handsome kinsman and welcomed the marriage. Young Trajan probably had no objections. The feel of a good sword and military strategies probably meant more to him than the look in a woman's eyes. Possibly his homosexuality had not surfaced as yet, and if he had to marry anyone Plotina would do. The marriage probably took place around 70.

Trajan served as a military tribune for ten years (Plin. *Pan.* 15. 10), a term of service unparalleled in the empire. He had a tour of duty in Syria where his father was legate (ibid., 14. 1) and probably in many of the armed provinces as well. Plotina must have remained in Rome, tending their property and running the household. In her leisure time, she probably read a great deal, especially philosophy. Indeed, she had need of it, for as the years passed and Trajan's preference for his own sex became more pronounced (Dio 68. 7. 4), Plotina must have been miserable. Her heart ached when Marciana, her sister-in-law, married and had a daughter. Undoubtedly, children would have filled her life, but she and Trajan remained childless.

Trajan's adoption by Nerva in 97 does not seem to have changed her quiet life. While he served as legate of Upper Germany, Plotina may have remained at home. Although it was permissible for the wife of an imperial legate to accompany her husband, Upper Germany was an unsettled province and Plotina probably did not find military life congenial. She may have continued her secluded life at Rome, for she must have been well aware that she could never rival the former empress,

Domitia, in either looks or poise. A portrait bust of her in the Vatican Museum reveals that she was very plain, her face gaunt and ascetic, with thin, drawn lips and a prominent nose. Her appearance is rather masculine, almost hard. A bust in the Metropolitan Museum of Art that may also be Plotina is somewhat more feminine, but her portraiture on coins bears out the impression of the Vatican bust.

However, her modesty was commendable. Dio records that when she first entered the imperial palace, she turned around so as to face the stairway and addressed the populace with the following words, "I enter here such a woman as I would fain be when I depart" (Cary 68. 5. 5). Dio also added that her conduct during the entire reign was blameless. This probably took place in 98 before Trajan's return to Rome. It may be guessed that Plotina was escorted to the palace by the most distinguished senators and matrons in Rome.

Pliny himself enthusiastically described Plotina as the model of antique virtue and modesty. His passage from the *Panegyricus* is eloquent (83. 4–8):

> For many men of rank a wife who has been taken
> with too little thought or retained with too great
> indulgence has been a cause of disgrace. Thus
> domestic shame destroyed fame abroad, and the fact
> that they were lesser husbands brought it about that
> they were not considered the most eminent citizens.
> Your wife goes forth for your honor and glory. What
> is more upright, more venerable than she is? If a wife
> had to be chosen by a chief pontiff, would he not have
> chosen her or someone similar to her? But where is
> one like her? She claims nothing from your good
> fortune except joy in it! How constantly she reveres,
> not your power, but you. Both are the same which
> you were. . . . How moderate she is in dress, how
> sparing in her retinue, how civil as she walks forth!
> This is the work of her husband who so imbued and
> instructed her, for the glory of obedience is sufficient

for a wife. . . . This would have befitted her if you acted in a different way, but truly considering this moderation of her husband how much modesty she owes, as a wife to her husband, as a woman to herself.

Pliny's connection with Trajan's family seems to have been only formal, but he has caught her character neatly here.

Pliny further noted that Plotina steadfastly refused the title of *Augusta* (84. 6). Plotina's image as a modest woman was also strengthened by the coinage issued in her honor. Her likeness is on the obverse, and· Vesta is depicted on the reverse. This association with the goddess who was the guardian of Rome's eternal fire and of each household hearth befits Plotina (*BMC* 3. 106–7, Nos. 525–28, Pl. 18. 12–14). Undoubtedly, she smiled when the Egyptians identified her with Aphrodite (*CIG* 3. 4716c). She eventually did accept the title of *Augusta*, but that was not until 104 or 105 (*ILS* 288).

Although Plotina appears to have had no hand in Trajan's administrative and military policies, she did possess considerable influence. The author of the *Epitome de Caesaribus*, desiring to demonstrate the contrast between the evil influence exercised by women over Constantius II and the good influence wielded by others, chose the example of Plotina. According to the anonymous author, Trajan's procurators were fleecing men from the provinces. Plotina, hearing of the matter, scolded her husband, for she regarded Trajan as forgetful of his good name. Whereupon her husband took heed (42. 20–21). It is very likely that this pleasant story is apocryphal, for Trajan is universally considered to have been an excellent administrator. However, the anecdote does contain some truth. Plotina appears to have known how to manage her husband by appealing to his vanity. And there is also her very humanitarian concern for justice.

This love of justice and concern for the oppressed

is borne out in some papyrus fragments in which details of an audience with Trajan are given (*POxy* 1242; Sm. 516). The Greeks and the Jews of Alexandria had sent delegations to Rome to present their side of the disturbances in that city between the two groups. Trajan is accused of being biased against the Greeks, while Plotina is charged with openly favoring the Jews.

However, Plotina must have found life at the imperial palace confining and boring. Trajan preferred the company of his marshalls. Marciana and her daughter, Matidia, were probably not great conversationalists. The empress must have been delighted by opportunities to travel, for there were certainly dedications in honor of the imperial family to attend, as well as journeys in her husband's retinue. She appears to have maintained an interest in literature and philosophy, for Pliny's literary friend, Voconius Romanus, sent her an enclosure (Plin. *Ep.* 9. 28. 1). She may have taken an interest in mathematics and music as well, for it is likely that "the best and most sacred of women" to whom the Pythagorean philosopher, Nicomachus of Gerasa, addressed his *Enchiridion Harmonicon* (Jan 242. 14) was Plotina. It would seem to be so, for the recipient of the tract was engaged in travel and her titulature is such that it seems to apply to a woman in the imperial family.

Plotina found unexpected pleasure in the friendship of Hadrian. He was young, handsome, brilliant, dashing, and impulsive. Plotina was impressed by his restless intellect, his thirst for knowledge. She may well have regarded him as the son she never had. Yet Hadrian did not get along with Trajan. It was basically a conflict of personalities. Trajan could not understand Hadrian's restless intellectual curiosity or passion for things Greek, while Hadrian may have regarded Trajan's quest of military glory as megalomania. Furthermore, Hadrian's youth and high spirits must have been a constant reminder to the aging emperor that his days were numbered. Yet Plotina sensed Hadrian's gifts and used her influence on his behalf. She urged his marriage with Trajan's grandniece, Sabina. Trajan appears to have opposed the match, although he eventually withdrew his objection (S. H. A. *Hadr.* 2. 10). He may have felt that Hadrian, who was overtly homosexual, would hardly be a proper husband for the lively and vivacious Sabina, and that his young grandniece was not fitted with Plotina's staid disposition to endure such a marriage. Plotina may have hoped that marriage might rid Hadrian of his homosexual urges. If so, she was wrong, for Sabina's marriage was dismal.

However, Plotina's influence did not stop with the marriage. Through her favor, Hadrian was appointed governor of Syria when Trajan undertook to conquer Parthia (S. H. A. *Hadr.* 4. 1). However, he was assigned no legions. Perhaps Trajan was afraid that Hadrian might gain glory, so eager was he to have the credit of victory. Plotina accompanied Trajan on his last campaign as far as Cilicia, perhaps through love of travel, perhaps because she knew that the emperor was not well and would not live much longer. Trajan left her in Hadrian's care, and when he returned, he was clearly dying (Dio 68. 33. 1). He managed to travel as far as Cilicia and then died. On his deathbed, it was said that he adopted Hadrian and named him as his successor, but the adoption was regarded with great suspicion. It was whispered that Plotina had concealed Trajan's death and smuggled in some individual to impersonate the dead emperor (Dio 69. 1. 2–4; S. H. A. *Hadr.* 4. 10). However, the story is unlikely. Probably Plotina did persuade Trajan to adopt Hadrian, when the emperor finally realized that he was dying. Hadrian was the best candidate with regard to birth and ability. The idea of the empress who was noted for her blameless character and integrity suddenly stooping to deception is out of character. Possibly such gossip was bruited about by enemies of Hadrian who opposed his accession and bitterly resented the execution of the four consular senators.

Her relationship with Hadrian caused considerable comment, for it was rumored that they were lovers (Dio 69. 1. 2; 10. 3). However, their relationship was almost certainly platonic. Trajan did not believe such a rumor, if it existed during his lifetime. He does not appear to have resented their friendship or credited it with any evil intent, for he would hardly have left his wife in Hadrian's care, if he had believed they were lovers. Letters that shed a great deal of light on their relationship survive. The first one is found in the *pseudo-dosithiana hermeneumata* that includes *Divi Hadriani sententiae et epistolae*. This letter from the emperor may be genuine or it may be an imperial pastiche. B. W. Henderson has rendered a charming translation of it:

> Greeting, my dearest and most honoured Mother!
> As you make many prayers to the Gods for me, so also I pray to Them for you. Your pity and honoured dignity achieve all things. I am glad, by Heracles, that everything I do pleases you and wins your praise.
> You know, Mother, that today is my birthday. We must have dinner together on my birthday. Please get ready and come with my sisters as early as you can. Sabina is away in the country, but she sent me her own birthday present. Come then, as quickly as you can, that we may spend the happy day together.

This letter, if genuine, would be dated after Hadrian's accession. It is definitely not the sort of letter that a man would write to his mistress, for it is full of filial piety and affection. Plotina's correspondence was no less proper. In 121, she petitioned Hadrian on behalf of Popillius Theotimus, then head of the Epicurean school at Athens. There was a ruling that the head of the school had to be a Roman citizen, and Plotina, who probably regarded herself as patroness of the school, asked that this ruling be remitted. The emperor was only too willing to grant her request. Plotina's letter and Hadrian's answer are in rather formal Latin. The third letter included in the inscription (Sm. 442) is in Greek and addressed to Theotimus and her Epicurean friends informing them of the decision. Here she was less formal and referred to Hadrian as (lines 21–23) "the benefactor and director of all education, most august emperor, to me most beloved in all matters, my lord and my good son."

After Trajan's death, Plotina returned to Rome with his ashes that were deposited in the base of Trajan's column (Dio 69. 2. 3; S. H. A. *Hadr.* 5. 9). She probably had no regrets about retiring into private life, for she could now be free from the confines of the imperial court. It may be guessed that her last years were pleasant ones. She could travel as she pleased, pursue her literary and philosophical interests, and perhaps even patronize authors of her choice. Hadrian must have visited her often and asked her advice, although she must have been disappointed that his marriage with Sabina proved unsatisfactory, that there would be no grandchildren for her to love.

Plotina died about 121 or 122. Hadrian grieved deeply, for he wore black for nine days, built a temple in her honor, and composed hymns in her memory (Dio 69. 10. 3). If he indulged in no theatrical displays of grief as he would when his adored favorite Antinous died, or made no lavish celebration of deification or issued coins to commemorate her death, it was probably because he felt his grief over his adopted mother's death was a private matter, not because he wished to silence any rumors over his own adoption or his relationship with Plotina. Furthermore, he had a precedent, for Tiberius, when Livia died, did not even attend her funeral and approved only a few of the honors that the Senate decreed to her memory and added that no religious worship was to be allowed, this having been his mother's own request (Tac. *Ann.* 5. 2. 1). However, Hadrian praised Plotina, saying, "Though she asked much of me, she was never refused anything." By this he simply meant to say: "Her requests were of such a character that they neither burdened me nor afforded me any justification for opposing them" (Dio 69. 10. 3^a). Dio's estimate is almost certainly correct. Hadrian's praise of her is as simple and ingenuous as her own character. Plotina as empress typified the old-fashioned virtues of a Roman matron. She was modest, dignified, and subject to her husband's wishes. Even in her philosophical interests she did not violate decorum.

SELECTED
BIBLIOGRAPHY

In Section A, most of the items are aimed at giving the student further knowledge of the period and are available in most college libraries. Three items are added as basic works used in comprising these chapters (Eck, *RE, PIR*). In B, the basic volumes are included for the more frequently cited literary sources. In C are included the works that identify references to the nonliterary sources. In D, we cite works on the content of individual chapters. *The American Journal of Philology* is abbreviated *AJP*, other journals are cited more fully.

A. Background of Early Imperial History

Bernoulli, J. J. *Die Bildnisse der roemischen Kaiser 2.* Stuttgart, 1891. Reprinted in 1969.

The Cambridge Ancient History 11 (1936). See especially chapters 1, 4 through 6, and 18 through 19.

Carcopino, J. *Daily Life in Ancient Rome* (English edition). New Haven, 1940. Now in paperback.

Crook, J. A. *Consilium Principis.* Cambridge, 1955.

Eck, W. *Senatoren von Vespasian bis Hadrian.* Munich, 1970.

Garzetti, A. *From Tiberius to the Antonines* (English edition). London, 1974. Full bibliography.

Groag, E., A. Stein, and Petersen, L. *Prosopographia imperii Romani.* 2d ed. Berlin, 1933ff (in press). For *nomina* A-L.

Hekler, A. *Greek and Roman Portraits.* New York, 1912. Reprinted in 1972.

McDermott, W. C. "Pliny the Younger and Inscriptions."

Classical World 65 (1971) :84–94 (hereafter referred to as "Pliny").

Orentzel, A. E. "Pliny and the Orators." Ph.D. diss., University of Pennsylvania, 1975 (*DA* 75. 14, 607).

The Oxford Classical Dictionary. 2d ed. Oxford, 1977.

Pauly-Wissowa, A. *Realencyclopaedie,* 1893ff (in press). For *nomina* M-V.

Salmon, E. T. *A History of the Roman World from 30 B.C. to A.D. 138.* 6th ed. London, 1968.

Scott, K. *The Imperial Cult under the Flavians.* Stuttgart, 1936. Reprinted in 1975.

Syme, R. "Pliny's Less Successful Friends." *Historia* 9 (1960) :362–79 (hereafter referred to as "Friends").

B. Literary Sources

Note: For abbreviations usually used in citing literary sources, compare *OCD*², pp. ix–xxii.

I. Josephus

Schuerer, F. *The History of the Jewish People in the Age of Jesus Christ* (English edition [with revisions and recent bibliography]). Vol. 1. Edinburgh, 1973. On Josephus, see especially pp. 43–63.

Thackery, H. St. J., and others. Loeb edition. 8 vols. 1926–1965.

II. Tacitus

Church, A. J., and Brodribb, W. J., trans. *The Complete Works of Tacitus.* Modern Library paperback.

Syme, R. *Tacitus.* 2 vols. Oxford, 1958.

III. Suetonius (*de vita Caesarum*)

Graves, R. *The Twelve Caesars.* Penguin, 1957. A vivid translation but often inaccurate. At times it seems a modernization of Rolfe.

Ihm, M., Leipzig. (*editio maior*). 1907. All citations are to this edition.

Mooney, G. W. Text, translation, and full notes on the last six lives. Dublin, 1930.

Rolfe, J. C. Loeb edition. 2 vols. Rev. 1928–1930. The text of Ihm is reprinted.

IV. Pliny the Younger

Mynors, R. A. B. *Epistulae*. Oxford, 1963.

————. *Panegyricus*. Oxford, 1964. All citations are to these two texts.

Radice, Betty. Translation of the letters. Penguin, 1963. Loeb translation of letters and panegryric. 2 vols. 1969. Reprinting the text of Mynors.

Sherwin-White, A. N. *The Letters of Pliny: A Historical and Social Commentary*. Oxford, 1966. Full commentary. In general his dating of the letters is followed.

V. Juvenal

Clausen, W. V. Text. Oxford, 1959.

Highet, G. *Juvenal the Satirist*. Oxford, 1955. Available now in paperback.

Humphries, Rolfe, trans. *The Satires of Juvenal*. Bloomington, 1958.

VI. Fronto

Haines, C. R. Loeb text. 2 vols. Rev. 1928–1929. This text is cited by volume and page.

VII. Cassius Dio

Cary, E. Volume 8 (1925) of the text and translation of the epitomes of Books 61–69 (covering A.D. 47–138). The numbering of book and paragraph follows Cary's arrangement in the Loeb edition, and where his translation is quoted his name is inserted.

Miller, F. *A Study of Cassius Dio*. Oxford, 1964.

C. The Nonliterary Sources

Note: A few items are cited below under individual chapters. Generally the most available or the most recent publication is cited.

AE: *L'année épigraphique*. 1888ff (in press). Cited by year and number.

BMC: H. Mattingly. *Coins of the Roman Empire in the British Museum*. Vols. 2–3. London, 1930, 1936. Cited by volume and page.

Selected Bibliography

CIL: *Corpus inscriptionum Latinarum*. Vols. 1–16. Berlin, 1863ff (in press). Cited by volume and number.

FO: *Fasti Ostienses*. In A. Degrassi, *Inscriptiones Italiae*. 13. 1 (Rome, 1947) Sec. 5. 173–241. Cited by fragment and line.

IGRR: *Inscriptiones Graecae ad res Romanas pertinentes*. Edited by R. Cagnat and G. Lafaye. Vol. 3 (1906), Vol. 4 (1927). Paris. Cited by volume and number.

ILS: H. Dessau, *Inscriptiones Latinae selectae*. 3 vols. Berlin, 1892–1916. Cited by number.

MW: McCrum, M., and Woodhead, A. G. *Select Documents of the Flavian Emperors*. Cambridge, 1961. Cited by number.

Sm: Smallwood, E. M., *Documents Illustrating the Principates of Nerva, Trajan, and Hadrian*. Cambridge, 1966. Cited by number.

D. Individual Chapters

I. Introduction

Note: These items are important for the revisionist version of Domitian.

Baldwin, B. "Themes, Personalities, and Distortions in Tacitus." *Athenaeum* 52 (1974):70–81.

Dorey, T. A. "Agricola and Domitian." *Greece and Rome* 7 (1960):66–71.

Hanfmann, G. M. A. *Roman Art*. Pp. 109–10. (The "Cancelleria Reliefs"). Greenwich, 1964.

Jones, B. W. "Preparation for the Principate." *Parola del Passato* 139 (1971):264–70.

———. "Domitian's Attitude to the Senate." *AJP* 94 (1973):79–91.

McDermott, W. C., and Orentzel, A. E. "Silius Italicus and Domitian." *AJP* 98 (1977):24–34, and "Quintilian and Domitian." *Athenaeum*. Forthcoming.

Orentzel, A. E. "Juvenal and Statius." *Classical Bulletin* 52 (1976):61–62.

Pleket, H. W. "Domitian, the Senate, and the Provinces." *Mnemosyne* 14 (1961):296–315.

Rogers, R. S. "A Group of Domitianic Treason Trials." *Classical Philology* 55 (1960):19–23.

Waters, K. H. "The Second Dynasty of Rome." *Phoenix* 17(1963):198–218.

——. "The Character of Domitian." *Phoenix* 18 (1964):49–77.

II. Fabricius Veiento

Jones, B. W. "Fabricius Veiento Again." *AJP* 92 (1971):476–78.

——. "The Dating of Domitian's War against the Chatti." *Historia* 22 (1973):79–90.

McDermott, W. C. "Fabricius Veiento." *AJP* 91 (1970):129–48. There are some revisions of the views expressed in this article.

——. "Plin. *Ep.* 4. 22." *Antichthon.* Forthcoming.

Scott, (*templum gentis Flaviae*), pp. 64–71.

IV. Berenice

Crook, J. A. "Titus and Berenice." *AJP* 72 (1951):162–75.

IG: Inscriptiones Graecae (*editio minor*). 1935. This volume is a shortened and revised edition of *CIG*, Vols. 2–3.

Jones, A. H. M. *Herods of Judea.* Oxford, 1938.

Maiuri, B. *Museo nazionali di Napoli* (Novara, 1957) 68 (cosidetta Berenice).

V. Fabatus

McDermott, "Pliny," pp. 84–85.

VI. Liberalis

Eck, (on Flavius Silva), p. 93–111.

McDermott, W. C. "Flavius Silva and Salvius Liberalis." *Classical World* 66 (1973):335–51.

VII. Corellius Rufus

Eck, (on proconsul of Asia), pp. 77–93.

McDermott, "Pliny," pp. 86–88.

VIII. Domitia

Bernoulli, Pl. 20. a–b, and compare pp. 62–66 and Pl. 21.

Selected Bibliography

Frank, T. *An Economic Survey of Ancient Rome.* 5 (Baltimore, 1940) : 207–9 (brickyards).

Hanfmann, G. M. A. *Roman Art* (Greenwich, 1964). See No. 76, p. 95 (text), p. 176 (plate).

Hekler, (Capitoline bust), Pl. 239b.

Scott, pp. 72–75, 83–87.

Syme, R. "Domitius Corbulo." *Journal of Roman Studies* 60 (1970) :27–39.

IX. Julia

Bernoulli, Pl. 15, and compare Pl. 16 and pp. 43–51.

Scott, (the gem with the apotheosis of Julia), pp. 75–78.

X. Regulus

Orentzel, A. E. "M. Aquilius Regulus." *Rheinisches Museum.* Forthcoming.

———. "The Critical Acumen of Pliny the Younger." *Classical Bulletin* 53 (1977) :65–68.

XI. Cornutus Tertullus

McDermott, "Pliny," pp. 88–91.

Syme, "Friends," pp. 362–64.

XII. Voconius Romanus

Syme, "Friends," pp. 365–67.

XIV. Euphrates

Bowersock, G. W. *Greek Sophists in the Roman Empire.* Oxford, 1969.

Grimal, P. "Deux figures de la correspondance de Pline : le philosophe Euphrates et le rheteur Isée." *Latomus* 14 (1955) :370–83.

Philostratus. *VA: Life of Apollonius of Tyana.* 2 vols. Loeb. Translated by F. C. Conybeare, 1912, 1950.

———. *VS: Lives of the Sophists.* Loeb. Translated by W. C. Wright. 1921.

XV. Pompeius Falco

McDermott, W. C. "*Quid stemmata faciunt* : The Descendants of Frontinus." *Ancient Society* 7 (1976) :229–61. See especially pp. 241–50.

Tudor, D. "Quintus Pompeius Falco." *Eunomia* 2 (1958) : 60–64.

Selected Bibliography

XVI. Plotina

Bernoulli, Pls. 29. a–b, 30, compare pp. 92–96.

CIG: Corpus inscriptionum Graecarum. Vol. 3. Berlin, 1853.

Hekler, Pl. 245b (the Vatican bust).

Henderson, B. W. *The Life and Principate of the Emperor Hadrian.* London, 1923. The Epicurean School (pp. 50–52) and the quotation from *pseudodositheus* (p. 185).

IC: M. Guarducci. *Inscriptiones Creticae.* Vol. 1. Rome, 1935.

McDermott, W. C. "Plotina Augusta and Nicomachus of Gerasa." *Historia* 26 (1977):192–203.

Richter, G. M. A. *Roman Portraits* (New York, 1948) 63 (profile and full-front: "perhaps Plotina").

Syme, R. "Hadrian the Intellectual." In *Les empereurs romains d'Espagne* (Paris, 1965):243–53.

Index

Index

The years from A.D. 70 to 177 represent a decisive period in the development of the Roman Empire. Thanks to the historians of the empire—Tacitus, Suetonius, Pliny the Younger, and others—we are familiar with the lives and personalities of the emperors who ruled during this time. But these classical sources say little of the people who played lesser roles in the affairs of the empire, although many were closely connected to the rulers and directly influenced their actions.

This book sketches the careers of fifteen men and women of the period from the ascension of Vespasian, the first Flavian emperor, to the end of Trajan's reign. The authors have drawn on inscriptional remains as well as classical history and biography to compile these useful portraits. The subjects are senators and soldiers, slaves, philosophers, and the wives, concubines, and siblings of the emperors. The book gives a unique view of the daily social and intellectual lives of the aristocracy of early imperial Rome.

In addition to its general appeal for aficionados of Roman history, *Roman Portraits* will interest scholars with its revisionist views of the